THE CELTIC SAINTS

By the same Author

WEST OVER SEA
ROCK OF TRUTH
IRISH PILGRIMAGE
IRELAND OF THE SAINTS
SCOTLAND OF THE SAINTS
THE ROADS FROM THE ISLES
THE MOUNTAINS OF IRELAND

THE CELTIC SAINTS

By

DAPHNE D. C. POCHIN MOULD

B.SC., PH.D.

NEW YORK

THE MACMILLAN COMPANY

1956

First Published 1956

Nihil obstat : JACOBUS CANONICUS BASTIBLE, Censor Deputatus
Imprimatur :   CORNELIUS, Episcopus Corcagiensis
    Die 4 Octobre, 1955

MADE AND PRINTED IN THE
REPUBLIC OF IRELAND BY
HELY'S LIMITED, DUBLIN.

DEDICATION

TO THE MOTHER OF MY PRINCE

ACKNOWLEDGMENTS

THE author wishes to thank the publishers of the translations from Irish sources for permission to quote them in this book. The Henry Bradshaw Society for the extracts from the Martyrology of Oengus, Irish Liber Hymnorum, Irish Litanies and Martyrology of Gorman. The Cambridge University Press for the extracts from the Thesaurus Palaeohibernicus. Messrs. Constable & Co. for Kuno Meyer's translation of the Hermit's Song. The Royal Irish Academy for extracts from *Eriu* (Kuno Meyer's translation of the poem on the Flightiness of Thought, R. I. Best's translation of the note on the Canonical Hours, extracts from Irish Rules). The extract from St. Augustine's *First Catechetical Instruction* is from the translation by J. P. Christopher in the Ancient Christian Writers series of the Newman Press, Maryland, and Messrs. Longmans, Green & Co. The extracts from John Cassian and St. Gregory the Great are from the Nicene & Post Nicene Fathers of the Church of the Oxford University Press series, and, from the same publishers, the extract from Kuno Meyer's translation of the Old Irish Commentary on the Psalms. The quotation from the Rule of St. Carthage and from the Leabhar Breac tract on the Mass is from the version in the Irish Ecclesiastical Record (1910, 1866). The translation of Moling's Hymn is from O'Hanlon's *Lives of the Irish Saints* (Burns Oates & Washbourne). The paragraph from St. Augustine's *De Doctrina Christiana* is from J. F. Shaw's translation, Edinburgh 1873. The literal translation of the Sancte Venite hymn is from Cardinal Moran's *Essays on the Early Irish Church* and that about the Rule of Bangor by W. Reeves (Ulster Journal of Archaeology, 1853). Portions of the material relating to the Celtic Breastplate, the Mass and Our Lady have appeared in *Doctrine & Life* and the editor is thanked for permission to reprint them.

FOREWORD

THE road by which I came to the writing of this book has been long and devious : from agnosticism to the Catholic Faith, from the Hebrides to Ireland, from the history of the Celtic Church to an impression of the character and outlook of the Celtic saints themselves.

It was this impression that remained with me after I had finished writing about the history of Celtic Ireland and Scotland, of the attractiveness, the charm, the integrity, of the Irish and Scottish saints, not as something that happened long ago, but as something relevant to us here and now.

So then, I have here attempted to outline, as best I could, something of the mind and outlook of the Celtic saints, especially of those of Ireland, for, as Manus O'Donnell wrote at the beginning of his *Betha Colaim Chille* (Life of St. Columcille), the honour of God, "the good of the folk that read" and to "the devil's dishonour and great hurt."

Contents

Chapter One

THE CELTIC SAINTS

SANCTITY is out and television is in. The city skyline is broken by the twisted arms of the TV aerial, not by the plain four-armed cross of Christ. TV is only a symptom of the disease of an age which has learned how to pull the atom to pieces without discovering how to integrate itself. It represents the immense technical and scientific achievement of the few for the enjoyment of the many : the dictatorship of a commercial technology which screams at us from every advertisement that progress is marked by new gadgets and that the secret of happiness is to be purchased with a washing machine and a new soap powder. And so we meekly do what the salesmen tell us is right, and buy the television set and sit watching the screen without making the first and most obvious enquiry, whether the screen is worth the watching at all.

Part of our troubles hark back to a steadily increasing urbanisation ; to the fact that more and more people are coming to live in large cities, in the ever-spreading jungle growth of tenement and shop. And the town dweller lives in a world of make-believe. It makes sense to tell the countryman that he is dust and will return to dust, when he has the mud clarted on his boots, but the townsman has discreetly veiled the earth that is his origin and support, with asphalt and paving stones, and does not know what you are talking about. The great city creates an environment in which man can imagine himself omnipotent, able to conquer darkness with street lights and to control the weather by going indoors out of the rain into a centrally heated building. Only at rare intervals need this make-believe city mentality be shaken, as when a war may force the realisation that somebody had to go out into the rain before the food got into the shops, and that the raw materials for the factory originated in a reality beyond the loaded trucks on the siding

And in the big town too, the sense of relation between the pattern of life and the pattern of work can so readily be lost, so that "work" is merely something to be got through for the sake of the pay packet and is never seen as something that is needed by the whole community. The countryman can see his job as a part of a definite and essential pattern : a multiplicity of city jobs seem only to be the means to annex more scientific toys with which to pass our leisure time away. It is not that factory work is necessarily duller or more repetitive than other kinds of work (there have been dull and repetitive jobs in plenty in all places and at all times), rather there seems a complete change in our set of values and philosophy, our interest is all in what we can get. The country too is being converted by the town to these beliefs, to the instinctive feeling that mechanical devices to save labour are the essential condition for the good life, and that existence without them is mere slavery.

It is not that these technical and scientific advances are not good in themselves, for they are ; it is our attitude to them, which tries to measure happiness by refrigerators and motor cars, which is in error. Long ago, St. Gregory the Great had described the complaint, the condition in which a man, whose mind can only find real rest in God, wanders from one thing to another, trying to make up for quality by variety. Yet, if we are honest with ourselves, we know that the variety would eventually pall on us : that if we could have an eternity of life on this earth and all that we desire to possess, and all the secrets of the material universe unravelled by research, we would be faced with a hell of boredom and despair, with the deadly monotony of the man-made Utopias.

Some indication that the city dwellers feel a sense of loss, and that the modern town's values are not the only ones, is shown by the great interest in the sport of mountaineering. The hard, high things are worth doing still, even if they bring no material reward, though the idea of a man risking his life in order to perch on a precarious leaf of rock on a mountain side is hardly explicable on the terms of the materialist philosophy of our technological civilisation. If he falls off, there is therefore not unnaturally an outcry about the need to control the rock climbers and save them from themselves and their sport.

In this environment of an increasingly pagan and materialistic culture, the idea of sanctity seems remote from the reality that most people know and touch, the bus passing the door, the spring fashions, the man to read the electric meter. Ours is a civilisation of specialists. The town's well-being depends on a few men with the know-how, the plumber and the electrician : the ordinary citizen goes about his own particular job with the comfortable feeling that if anything goes wrong with his amenities he can telephone for the appropriate "man" to come and put it right for him. Rather naturally, therefore, if the ordinary citizen regards the idea of sanctity as anything more than a mental disease or, at best, a mild form of crankiness, he regards it as a specialist job— not as the one thing which could unify and direct the whole of his own life. We think that we need to make a choice, saint or scientist, contemplative or air hostess, not that the one vocation should embrace and direct the other, that the plumber ought also to be a man of prayer. Yet the salvation of the modern city seems to rest on just such a re-orientation of its values and a directing back of its outlook to God. And that will not be achieved by a few of its citizens flying into the desert ; it demands that the politician and the bus driver and the boy who leaves the milk should integrate their lives and their work and direct them to God and be themselves saints.

It is in this context that I rather tentatively dig up the past and try to map the mechanics of the sanctity of the Celtic saints. For they do appear to have brought this business of integrating diverse elements into a unity of holiness to a fine art, and it seems possible that we may be helped by their methods. This is no harking back to some idyllic Arcadia : the world of the Celtic Church,* from its beginnings with the mission of St. Ninian in Scotland and St. Patrick in Ireland in the 5th century to St. Malachy's introduction of the Cistercians to Ireland in the 12th, was that of the Europe which experienced all the distress of the break-up of the Roman Empire, and the Ireland and Scotland that felt the shock of the Viking attacks and suffered their own private quota of war and intrigue between their own network of little states. Men's passions and vices are unchanging through the ages : it has always been desperately hard to be a saint.

Nor did the Celtic saints fly from the troubles of the world in which they found themselves to the desert of mountain or island ; the "desert" retreat was rather the springboard for action. Our specialist technology leads us to think that the saint must be an enclosed nun : the Celtic

*The term "Celtic Church" is a convenient one to distinguish that part of the Catholic Church established in countries whose people spoke one or other of the Celtic languages (Ireland, Scotland, Wales). The Catholic Faith is universal, yet adaptable to each nation's personality. So, in using the name Celtic Church, I am not presupposing some long dead individualistic Church, but am referring to the Catholic Church in Celtic countries over the period from the arrival of its first missionaries there until about the time of the Anglo-Norman invasion of Ireland.

THE CELTIC SAINTS

saints made no such dichotomy in their ideas, they succeeded in being both saints and politicians, in combining the life of prayer and contemplation with that of action, of preaching and teaching and adventurous exploration. The intention of this book is to try to indicate the outlines of the history and achievement of this dynamic Celtic sanctity.

Chapter Two

THE DESERT

THE broad farmlands of eastern Scotland fronting the Moray Firth have a charm all their own; at their back the line of the Highland mountains, the clouds piled above them and the snow lingering into summer in their corries, and, on the other hand, the constant line of the sea, blue, flecked with white or grey and menacing. The lowland beside the sea is fertile country and among the many snug and pleasant settlements there is that of Nigg, an old graveyard, a few houses, tucked in on a level flat, a low hill to break the snell winds off the North Sea to the east of it, and, to the west, the land falling to the sandy inlet of Nigg Bay. Within the churchyard is preserved a great carved cross slab of the Celtic Church, elaborate with Celtic interlace and ribbon beasts and the strange symbols of the eastern inhabitants of Scotland of those times, the Picts. At the top of the slab, two old men bend down in adoration before a chalice, above which a bird descends holding a round piece of bread in its beak.

And with that carving, the Celtic artist takes us back to stark essentials; the mind turns from the comfortable farmland and from the urbanity and civilisation represented by the ornate knots and twists of the Celtic designs, and leaps the seas to the bare sands and rocks of the desert and the wild and perilous adventure of the beginning of monasticism there.

If you follow the Celtic saints through Scotland and Ireland and study the great high crosses of the Celtic Church sites, of which Nigg is an example, you will again and again come upon this picture, the two old hermits and the bread from heaven, or, another part of the same story, a man standing alone and attacked on either side by devils whose bodies are those of women but whose heads are those of birds. The pictures occur almost monotonously on the high crosses (9th-10th

15

centuries) and on the more primitive cross pillars that preceded them. The great cross of Ruthwell in the south of Scotland shows the two hermits and there each picture has its title inscribed alongside : they are St. Paul, the first hermit, and St. Anthony, the father of Christian monasticism. The other picture, the man attacked by demons, is of St. Anthony's temptation when he was alone in his desert retreat.

It all seems very far away, the hermit monks of the eastern deserts and St. Jerome's story of St. Anthony seeking out the elder hermit, Paul, and the bird flying down with the loaf of bread for their meal together. We smile at the fancy of the story, the simple Paul pleased that the friendly crow should bring a whole loaf instead of the half one that it normally brought the old man each day when he was alone. Perhaps the Nigg artist smiled too, for it is a pleasant story and one to go straight to the heart of the Celtic monks who loved animals, but if he did enjoy the tale as a tale, he saw a deeper and more urgent symbolism beneath the fancy. He showed the two old men bowed to the ground and left no room for doubt that here was a symbol of the Mass, of the bread from heaven that had been foreshadowed by the manna coming down upon the Israelites wandering through the desert. The Nigg carving is not only of Anthony and Paul, it is of all Christians, it is the illustration of one of the communion antiphons of the 7th century Antiphonary of Bangor, the oldest surviving Celtic liturgical book :—

"Hic est panis vivus qui de coelo descendit, Alleluia.
Qui manducat ex eo vivit in aeternum. Alleluia."

(This is the living bread that came down from heaven. He that eateth this bread shall live for ever.)

So, in the fertile country of Nigg, we come upon three of the basic foundations of the Celtic Church, the desert fathers and the desert wisdom that was the basis of Celtic monasticism, indeed of all Christian monasticism ; the Celtic devotion to the Mass and to the Blessed Sacrament ; and the Celtic sense of symbol and symbolism. They are fundamental themes of Catholic Christianity everywhere, but all three are hard for the ordinary post-Christian man in the street to grasp. We have no sympathy with the desert monks as an historical fact, and the concept of the desert as a symbol of something that happens to each one of us is meaningless. Yet the Nigg cross, set amongst the farmlands, points the way back to the desert.

For us, the desert already means two things. It may mean mirage, the glitter of unreality. Or it may mean clear skies and clear sun, rock and sand baking in the heat, the glitter of reality. But whichever way we look at the desert, there is a tinge of savageness in its beauty; only the essentials remain, all the cushioning of civilisation is shorn away. Here life must be lived in its basic essentials; reality is sun and sand-storm, water and bread.

We see the desert as the land of mirage, a place to which the early hermits and monks fled because they could not face the reality and responsibility of life in the city and with their fellow men. For us, it is the mirage of the starved ascetic whose fevered imagination conjures up visions of devils; the mirage of God that the sick mind sees in contemplation.

Indeed and the devil spoke for all of us when he tempted Christ in the desert, "If you are the Son of God, command that these stones be made bread." We too cry out for results, the tangible obvious results that our scientists labour to give us. The sun glitters on the desert sands, if the power of God really exists it might so easily do something useful for us and turn the useless stones into candy and cake. And so we take our stand with the devil and repeat the old taunt with endless variations : "If you are the Church of God, command that men no longer oppress one another, command that wars end, command that social injustice be taken away, command that the innocent no longer suffer."

But the answer is still the same. "Man does not live by bread alone, there is life for him in all the words that proceed from the mouth of God."

It is an idiotic answer as every practical man will tell you; the answer of a starved dreamer in the wilderness. For indeed we do live by bread alone, these are our basic needs, the wage packet, meals and smokes and drinks, house and furniture; only when these are comfortably supplied do we think of seeking a little intellectual amusement by dabbling in religion or philosophy. These things are for the leisured, they are hardly basic for humanity.

It was the same dreamer who put the challenge in another way, the challenge of the desert, and said that it was easier for a camel to get through the eye of a needle than for a rich man to enter the kingdom of heaven. The rich man indeed is not particularly keen upon entering heaven anyway, his heaven is already about him, bought with his riches, and the road to the other heaven passes through the desolation of the desert.

There was a rich man once, however, who saw the matter differently and gave up his riches and his city life and his comfortable civilisation, and set out to wander the desert. His name was Abraham.

He did not go, as a practical and sensible individual would, on the substantiated report of something better to be got elsewhere brought him by other reliable men. He went because God told him to go, to leave home and kinsfolk and seek the land which God would show him, *Tír Tairngiri* of the Irish Celtic writers, the Land of Promise. Abraham took God for Truth and went off into the desert, as Anthony was to do centuries later, suddenly moved by the gospel's advice to the rich man, "If thou wilt be perfect, go sell all that thou hast, and give it to the poor ; and come, follow me and thou shalt have treasure in heaven."

It is a savage and fanatic act of faith, this leaving of the tangible good around for the intangible *Tír Tairngiri*, trusting the word of a God whose very existence the modern world seems to call in question. It is as savage and wild as the desert itself, the adventurer blinded by the wind-driven sand and the sun blotted out ; the desert of thirst and hunger, of water miraculously struck from the rock and bread falling from heaven. Yet the *Life of St. Columcille* in the Book of Lismore begins by telling the story of God's command to Abraham to go on pilgrimage to the Land of Promise and immediately goes on to point out that this same act is incumbent upon all the Christian faithful, spiritual sons of Abraham "to leave their country and their land, their wealth and their worldly delight, for the sake of the Lord of the Elements, and to go into perfect pilgrimage in imitation of him." And Columcille, who might have been High King of Ireland, took that path and preached Christ over Ireland and the western seaboard of Scotland.

The desert then is a symbol of something that is going to happen to every Christian, if he is true to his calling. The Old Testament figures the pattern, the Red Sea that the Israelites crossed as a symbol of baptism, then the wandering in the desert and only at the very end, the coming to the Land of Promise. Only a very few traverse the real desert that Anthony and Paul knew, but the things that the desert symbolises are for all and each of us. First, that almost insane looking faith in God, the certainty that He exists and that He is Truth and that we can trust Him completely and entirely. And secondly, that this same God is infinitely lovable, so much so that we must detach ourselves from all the clinging lovely things that He has created, so that by loving their Creator first, we can come back to His creation and delight in it as free men, no longer tangled and confused by its variety. It is the Christian paradox about the man who saves his life by losing it, and that is a hard road. The other panel from the life of St. Anthony on the high crosses which shows his temptation, stands for something very real and very terrible. There is no compromise in the desert, the stakes are life and death, and the attacks upon us come in a multitude of forms and disguises, as did the demons upon Anthony.

Meantime, we need to look closer at the origins and history of the monks who went into the real desert. They themselves looked back to the Old Testament for the origins of their manner of life, to Elias and Eliseus, and also to John the Baptist. But this was an afterthought, the real origins seem to have been a seeking for a closer union with God and a more perfect form of life, an attempt to put the counsels of the gospels of poverty and chastity and obedience into practice. Men and women had been so doing from the very start of the gospel being preached, but the movement gradually became more organised and fixed in its directions, persecution slackened and perhaps men began to seek for other ways to gain the prize that had been earlier bought with the martyrs' blood. If St. Jerome's little biography of St. Paul, the first hermit, is based on fact, that individual was one of the first to seek an ascetic life in the wilderness, but the real originator of the movement, who, by his own teaching and example and by the widely read *Life* written by his friend, St. Athanasius, set the fire of monasticism really alight, was St. Anthony.

We think of the desert monks as crazy fanatics, men driven mad by wild penances, circled by demons of their own illusions. It is a shock to read St. Athanasius' account of Anthony, for here is a man who did all the wild things, lived alone in the desert, eating the absolute minimum, fighting the devils; yet a man who charmed all he met, a rational and balanced individual with outstandingly shrewd good sense.

Anthony was born c. 250, probably at the town of Coma in Middle Egypt. His people owned a decent holding of land, a farm of nearly 300 acres, and when his parents died, the property passed into Anthony's hands, for his own support and that of his younger sister. Anthony was then about 20, brought up Christian, for his parents had been Christian too, a zealous church-goer, but with little schooling—he could not read. Like all countrymen with little book learning, he took in what he heard all the more effectively and remembered the readings from the scriptures which he heard. It was in church that he was suddenly struck by the force of Christ's advice to the rich young man, to sell all that he had, and Anthony at once set about doing so ; selling the farm, and after a little hesitation about keeping back some of the money obtained for his sister's maintenance, giving this away also, placing the girl in the keeping of some women ascetics, who seem to have formed a primitive nunnery in the district, and himself turning completely to follow Christ in penance and poverty.

He proceeded cautiously, moving about the district and visiting other ascetics already famous, staying with them and learning from each what he had to teach. Only when he had gained all he could by this research did he launch out alone to face the temptations and hardships of the desert by himself. Eventually, he found out a deserted fort at a place named Pispir and spent about twenty years there by himself. But the hermit who attains any sort of sanctity is never left alone in peace ; men began to come to the old fort and to break in on Anthony's solitude, to learn from him and copy his life. Very soon, Anthony found himself at the head of a group of hermits. The movement grew, and Anthony had to become leader and teacher and adviser of these eager men who came flocking into the wilderness. Not only disciples but the sick came to him, asking for his prayers and help. When the persecution of Christians under Maximin Daja took place, the hermit went to the city of Alexandria, to help those who were executed or imprisoned and to take the chance of martyrdom himself. However, he survived to go back to the desert and there try to get away from the crowds that surrounded him, by going to the "Inner Mountain," Dêr Mar Antonios. Here he discovered a pleasant retreat, a date palm and a spring and a nook of land that could be watered from the well and cultivated. To begin with, his disciples brought him a supply of bread at intervals, but the old man thought this was putting them to too much trouble and asked instead for a hoe, axe and a bag of seed, so that he could raise his own crop of corn. Later, the little garden was planted with vegetables—so that the hermit could offer some variety of refreshments to his visitors. At first, the plot was raided by animals, then the saint caught one and told it that it should not harm his garden when the saint was doing no harm to the wild creatures himself. From then on his plot was left unmolested.

Anthony died in 356, at the age of 105—a dramatic reminder to those who imagine that austerity and asceticism will injure their health! His lifetime had seen the first tentative movement of hermits into the desert become a torrential flood, a flood that Anthony's example and teaching had guided and controlled. Two movements had come into being in the desert, the hermits who lived either alone or grouped round a leader like Anthony, yet still hermits, meeting only in the church on Saturday and Sunday, or when gathered round their leader to receive instruction from him at intervals. The other movement was monastic, the idea of a community who worked and prayed together as a community, and its origins go back to the foundation of Tabennisi of Pachomius. Pachomius was born c. 290 and was a pagan, but was converted to Christianity by the example of some Christians who gave food and comforts to some passing soldiers, of whom Pachomius was one. When he left the army, he too went off into the desert, but organised his followers there into a definite community, following a definite programme in common. This too attracted enormous numbers, and soon fresh monastic groups had to be formed from the overcrowded nucleus at Tabennisi. Women joined in the movement and Pachomius' sister seems to have led in founding a series of nunneries. Pachomius died in 346, ten years before Anthony. And though Pachomius was the founder of the kind of monasticism that was to become the norm of all later Christian monasticism, it is Anthony who towers above all the other early hermits and monks, and Anthony whom the Celtic high crosses almost monotonously represent.

Anthony's fame was spread by the biography written by his friend, St. Athanasius, probably composed in the year following Anthony's death. To the modern reader, Athanasius' little book comes as a curious blend of hard-headed good sense and peculiar and fantastic stories about devils. Here are all the things that strike us as odd or even completely insane, the austerity, the savage fasts, the vigils, the struggles with temptations in the visible form of devils. If that was all, we might write it off as sheer madness, except for the fact that a lunatic does not start a powerful movement like that of the Christian monks and hermits, a movement moreover which appealed to all classes and sorts of men. Yet the fantastic part is only half the story, Anthony's spiritual teaching and general behaviour is not of a man gone crazy with solitude and penance, but of a man very wise and very level-headed.

Anthony had a lot of the countryman's habit of thought, the trick of mulling over things in his mind and then bringing out a totally unexpected line of reasoning to confute the city men who had come out to poke fun at the old hermit. He got the better of two Greek philosophers who came to see him ; one can meet Scottish crofters who would use exactly the same technique. He asked them why they had gone to the bother of coming to see a foolish old man ? Naturally, the Greeks had to say that he was not foolish at all but very wise. "Well, then," said Anthony, "if I am foolish, you've gone to a lot of trouble to no purpose, but if I am really wise, then you should imitate me." He pointed out that we should always imitate the good, as he, Anthony, would have done, if he had gone to see the Greek philosophers as they had come to see him, and that they should therefore set about so doing, and become Christians.

Another group came to jeer at his lack of schooling and ignorance of letters. So he asked them which came first, mind or letters? They admitted that mind was first and had invented letters, giving Anthony the splendid opportunity to point out that therefore a man with a sound mind had no essential need of letters.

But these things were only Anthony's way of dealing with tiresome visitors, and getting a little quiet fun out of them: the teaching that he gave to the hermits gathered round about him came from much deeper springs. He taught them to put complete confidence in God and to love Him; to avoid evil thoughts and the pleasures of the flesh, to pray continually and to sing the Psalms both before they slept and when they woke, to learn the commandments of scripture by heart so that they could meditate on them, to study the examples of the saints. He warned them to avoid sinning and to keep a daily check on their actions, so that if they had sinned, they could stop doing so, and if they had not, avoid boasting of it. He seems to have advocated actually listing one's sins at this daily examination of conscience on the principle that nobody likes to be seen doing wrong in public, so the written report could stand, as it were, for the eyes of the other hermits and shame the individual into doing better in future. Especially he advised to live each day as if it was our last, lying down to sleep as if we should not waken, getting up and setting about the day's work as though we should not see the evening. It is advice we could all well take, for it keeps the right sense of proportion: face to face with eternity, the petty annoyances of the neighbours, the passing worries, fall into their proper place and cease to overshadow our lives.

All this sounds very sane, and almost commonplace, a long way from the high cross carving of the hermit and the two devils. But Anthony told his monks too about his visions of devils and their temptations, not to boast of his experience, but to show them how to deal with such happenings. His attitude is neither credulous nor superstitious: the grace of Christ is sufficient to deal with all their wiles, whether they tempt by suggesting evil thoughts, or appearing in terrible and fantastic forms, or, a peculiarly cunning temptation, urging the hermit on to excessive piety, wearing him out by rousing him up to more prayers each time he tried to get some sleep. Nor need the monks take any notice of the devils' apparent power to foretell future events; Anthony, level-headed countryman, saw through this particular manifestation readily enough. He said that the devils often forecast the Nile floods, anybody could do the same that had information about the rainfall in the district of the headwaters and who could move quickly enough to get well ahead of the movement of the water. So, too, they often told of visitors coming to see the hermits, which anybody with greater speed could do, once they saw the people setting out on their journey. Sometimes the devils were taken in themselves, for the people changed their direction or their intentions and did not arrive where they were expected to!

Anthony gave a simple test to distinguish devilish from heavenly visions. Visions of devils or conjured up by devils—for the devils tried to appear as Christ, or as angels—are noisy, turbulent and accompanied by fear; the ascetic experiences depression and dejection and a hatred of virtue. But heavenly visions bring quiet and peace and a greater urge to do good—even if we are frightened at the beginning, this soon passes, for the fear is driven out by love, just as the angels told the shepherds in the Gospel story, "Fear not." So, too, said Anthony, Abraham rejoiced when he saw the Lord, and John the Baptist leaped in his mother's womb for joy at hearing the voice of Mary, the Mother of God.

We cannot understand either the historic desert and its monks, or the reality in each Christian's life that is symbolised by the desert, unless we face these articles of Anthony's teaching. And they are out of step with the tempo of modern life; we do not naturally go about our work or play facing the thought of death, nor do we imagine a host of demons waiting to pounce upon us. We get out of the difficulty by supposing that the demons are merely an illusion, and that the stress of keeping one's attention on eternity and not this life of time and space is an escape from reality, a refusal to face up to facts.

Yet it is not so easy to write off the demons as mere illusion in Anthony's life, quite apart from the fact that their existence forms part of the Christian revelation. Undoubtedly each age has its literary conventions and when St. Athanasius wrote, his readers wanted stories of demons and miracles, and he accordingly put them into the book and made the most of them. This is not our literary convention—we go to the opposite extreme and instead of demanding that our heroes appear very extraordinary, want them to appear very ordinary. This has been called the "Age of the Common Man" and we like to think

that our heroes are just the same as ourselves but for lucky circumstances. Biographers stress their ordinary home life and ordinary interests,
and probably do as much violence to facts as did mediaeval hagiographers
with their lists of miracles and wonders. Perhaps the modern biographer,
who plays down the extraordinary, does the more harm, when he comes
to deal with the saints, for they are undoubtedly uncommon men, the
salt of the earth, with a tang about them that does not belong to the
rest of us.

But when you have allowed for the literary convention of St.
Athanasius' times, something remains to make the Temptation of
Anthony on the high crosses stand for something more than a mere
fairy tale. Anthony was too sane and too shrewd in other ways to be
taken in by the visions of delirium. He did indeed face a long series
of very various temptations alone in the desert; perhaps some of them
did appear as actual visions. What is more, the Anthony that emerged
from the solitude and the temptations, was a more mature and wiser
Anthony than had faced them at the start. It is the old story about
the Christian's warfare against the world and the flesh and the devil,
and the soldier who puts his whole trust in God emerges from the
conflict a seasoned and resourceful campaigner.

And for better or for worse, these things are the preoccupation of
the Celtic saints, indeed of all Christian saints: the wide horizon of
the desert and its haunting spirits. For to live as if facing death each
moment is to live looking out on a wide horizon, for it is to live facing
eternity, and to see one's whole life and the world around one in the
light of eternity and of God. If God and eternity exist, it is an enormous
liberation of the human soul. It is both a reaching out into infinity and
a setting of the material world about us in order, a seeing of life in its
proper perspective. So, too, the belief in pure spirits, whether angel or
devil, is a widening of horizons, not a shutting in by superstition. If
they exist, to know about them, to make friends with the angels and
fight with the devils is, at the very least, an enlargement of our knowledge
of the real world, which we all admit we want to have.

And even if we deny the existence of God and of the angels and the
devils, it still appears that for those who do believe life is going to be
both more simple and more adventurous. Simpler, because men like
Anthony knew where they were trying to go and to whom they were
trying to get; more adventurous, because to them each incident of life
was part of a pattern, of the pilgrimage route to the Land of Promise,
and therefore to be dealt with in the spirit of a pilgrim adventurer,

almost of a knight errant, rather than that of the modern to whom things just happen without purpose or meaning.

It is to this wide outlook on life, this sense of the all-importance of God, that the lichened Celtic crosses, with their stiff figures showing the two old hermits in the desert, bear witness. Celtic litanies take up the theme, invoking Anthony and the "troop of monks" that came to follow the trail he had blazed. The Celtic writers of the litanies saw Anthony as the leader of all the monks in heaven, almost like the chieftain of a Scottish clan: they asked his help to guide them on the same road across the desert.

Chapter Three

THE WISDOM OF THE DESERT

SET on a grassy hill overlooking the sparkling sea inlet of Bantry Bay in the south-west of Ireland, the mountains rising in a rugged line beyond the water, is a thin pillar stone of the Celtic Church. On the one side, a figure stands praying, hands uplifted to heaven, below is a cross, and underneath this again, Anthony and Paul in the desert. The carving on the opposite face is nearly weathered away but has been made out to be the ship of the Church, shown sailing heavenwards out of a sea of little crosses. Perhaps we can read into these carvings the connection between the desert and the hermits and the body of learning about the spiritual life that they put together, and the way that their teaching came to be made use of by the Celtic saints. For the books that were written and the stories that circulated about the desert monks and hermits, and that came into Celtic Ireland and Britain, were not only about the historical or legendary happenings in the wilderness, but about how one should pray and how the ship of the Church and of the individual soul, might be steered to the Land of Promise.

Of the writers about the teaching of the desert monks and hermits, the outstanding figure is John Cassian. He was born c. 360, and, after receiving a good education, entered a monastery at Bethlehem. From there, he went off into the Egyptian desert and spent many years living with the monks and hermits there and learning all that he could from them about the Christian way of life that they were practising. Later, about 403, he went to Constantinople, where he made friends with St. John Chrysostom, by whom he was ordained deacon. He supported St. Chrysostom in the various attacks made on him, and took news of these affairs to Rome where he was ordained a priest. Eventually, he settled at Marseilles about 410, where he founded a monastery and also a convent for women. By his own life he was therefore an important

link in the bringing of monasticism into the West, but his influence
extended much further than his mere physical perambulations by virtue
of his two books about the monastic life. The first of these was written
at the request of a certain Bishop Castor, of Apta Julia, forty miles to
the north of Marseilles. This bishop wanted to introduce the monastic
way of life to his diocese and asked Cassian for information about the
rules followed by the Egyptian monks. The result of this request was
the *De Institutione Coenobiorum*, on the Institutes of the Coenobia. Later,
Cassian followed up this first work with another and longer one about
the teaching of the various eminent men he had met in the desert, the
Collationes Patrum, the Conferences. This second book was finished by
the year 428 ; Cassian himself died in 435.

John Cassian's influence upon Western Europe was immense and
long lasting. His writings sum up all the teaching about the spiritual
life that had come into being and matured in the first four centuries
of Christianity. He belongs to the great tradition of writers who have
not only travelled to see the people they write about and interviewed
them carefully and sympathetically, but who have stayed with them
long enough to live their life and really learn from them. His Conferences
are therefore no series of slick reportings of a lightning tour through
the desert ; rather they are John Cassian looking for truth and trying
to help others in the same search. St. Thomas Aquinas is said to have
read a portion of the Conferences each day, and to dip into them is
to fall under the same spell, for this is no book about fantastic happenings
in a faraway land, but one about men and God, and how men may
come to know God and know themselves and their faults. It is a shrewd
analysis of human nature : it comes almost as a humiliating shock to
us to discover how deeply these old men in the desert that Cassian
sought out had penetrated human nature.

But before singling out some of the important points made by
Cassian's desert friends, it is as well to remember that the cross on the
Bantry pillar stone, set between the praying figure and St. Paul and
St. Anthony, stands for more than a mere pious symbol. It is not only
a sign of victory over sin and death, but it is also a reminder of
something that happened in history : that Christianity is not a theory
but is tied up with a series of historical events. To suppose that the
desert ascetics were running away from reality in search of a philosophical ideal is to misunderstand them completely, because the whole
basis of their faith is thirled to a series of events taking place in time,
and relating to real people : Adam and Eve turned out of paradise,

God incarnate in a Virgin's womb, a particular cross outlined against a particular sky, the shocking impossibility of the Resurrection on the first Easter morning.

Men who look for a vague and comfortable faith will not find it in Christianity, any more than they will find comfort and vagueness in the desert itself. Christianity is something definite and dogmatic, and must be from its very nature, because it is concerned with this man, this woman, this place, and not that other man or place.

The key word in the whole system is charity, God's love for man. The Christian believes in a God Who, although perfectly self-sufficient and happy in Himself, created the world and man out of superabundant goodness, intending to bring man to the beatific vision of God in heaven for all eternity. Man, however, was given free-will, and in the person of Adam chose to rebel against God and to forfeit heaven. From the human point of view, the position was irretrievable : it is the shepherd who must take the initiative in rounding up the strayed sheep. The answer of the love of God to the problem was the coming of Christ to men, the Incarnation, Christ Who is both God and the way back to God. The initiative remains always with God ; it is He Who loves us first, and to His love that we try to respond. In point of fact, it is hard to even begin to understand what God's love for us is like, to even come near the dynamic force that brought Christ to the cross for our sakes. If we do begin to get this understanding, it follows that the most important thing in life is to try and come to know and love God better, that the contemplation of God in prayer is the highest form of human activity.

Nobody gets blamed for running after a beautiful woman, or for wanting a car or a house or a million dollars. But they do get blamed if, instead of running after some particular and material good thing, they run after the source of all these particular goods, Goodness itself. The man who wants to find God in silence and solitude is called crazy, or, at the very least, anti-social. Yet the love of God is the one thing that cannot be selfish and anti-social, for each Christian, wherever he may be, is a member of the mystical body of Christ in a close spiritual link-up which transcends time and space. The hermit praying alone in the desert is able to help the men crowded in the cities ; just as the still mountain pools feed the reservoirs that power the hydro-electric plants.

But, "Quis ascendet in montem Domini ? aut quis stabit in loco sancto ejus ? Innocens manibus et mundo corde' (Who shall go up to the mountain of the Lord : or who shall stand in his holy place ? The innocent in hands and the clean of heart). (Psalm 23).

The route to the heights is indicated by a sentence in the early 9th century Irish "Rule of St. Carthage" :—

"It is the way to the kingdom of the Prince—noble is its virtue, love of God with the whole soul, with heart and deed."

But, like all climbs, the ascent of the mountain of the Lord involves several different things. The mountaineer stands in the valley and looks up to the summit, to the serrate ridge of rock, etched with flashing cornices of snow, outlined against the blue of the sky, and to that high rock, his heart goes out. But between the valley in the shadow of the hillside and the sunlit crest lies all the adventure and all the toil of the climb up, the squelching bog, the stony sheep path, the scree run, rough rock with a hold for boot nail and finger tip. The way up is by all these different kinds of conflict, but the climber must first meet a different and more personal conflict—with himself. To climb to the heights, the mountaineer must have a reasonable degree of physical fitness, and, further, have the kind of control of himself that will keep him going up when most of his instincts will want to make him turn back and go down. He must know how to overcome weariness and fear—most especially if he climbs alone—and be able to look steadily upon the sudden drop of the precipice up which he makes his way.

The same problems face the Christian : his objective is to climb up to God, but to do so, he must not only set his heart upon his objective and deal with the problems that crop up between him and it, but he must also get himself into condition if he is to succeed in his attempt. This is the first objective of Christian asceticism ; the desert monks were not trying to destroy the body but to get it into a reasonable state of health. The Christian conflict with the flesh is constructive and not destructive in reality. Before the Fall, there had been a nicely graded hierarchy in which man, subject to God, had himself and his passions equally subject to his will and intellect ; after the Fall, the rebellion against God left him hoist with his own petard in that he was no longer in proper control of himself. Baptism remits the guilt of this original sin of ours, but the weakness that the sin produced remains, just as a sick man may be cured of his complaint and yet need a long period of convalescence.

The problem therefore, of both gaining a proper control of ourselves and rooting out our particular sins and failings, is crucial : it is only the pure of heart who will see God. So John Cassian gives up a considerable amount of space to the subject, distinguishing eight principal faults, as against the list of seven deadly sins with which we are more familiar. It is interesting to follow up Cassian's influence and this eightfold division into Ireland, where the same classification is found in the Penitential of Cummean, the son of King Fiachna of West Munster, which was written c. 650. The eight faults are:—gluttony, fornication, covetousness, anger, dejection, accidie (sloth), vainglory and pride. The list conjures up at first a mental image of a line of gargoyles on a Gothic cathedral, each representing a particular sin, the titles sound remote, unreal, until we begin to read what Cassian has to say about them and discover what we today so much tend to forget, the unchanging character of human nature. Our instincts and our failings are the same as those of the first desert hermits.

The spirit of gluttony is the first of the group that Cassian deals with, the spirit of the pig replete beside its trough. For he says that until we get control of ourselves in this matter, we cannot go on to root out the other vices. It is not only food for the body that we need to fast from and use in moderation, but those other harmful foods of the mind, slander and anger and envy and the like. Yet if we imagine that the standards of the desert in fasting and abstinence were fantastic and beyond the normal individual's achievement, Cassian's balanced phrases give that idea the lie; purity and chastity do depend on keeping to a balanced and moderate diet, but circumstances must determine for each one of what kind and how much the diet is to be. He points out that even the physically weak can always do something: "wherefore as no state of life can be deprived of the virtue of abstinence, so to none is the crown of perfection denied."

Prayer is the way in which we keep in touch with God, both in getting to know Him better and asking for help in all our difficulties. It ought to be continuous, as continuous as breathing, and the desert monks tried to maintain this permanent link-up with God. There were fixed hours of formal, liturgical prayer: the beginning of the Church's Divine Office, and between-whiles, the monk kept his mind on God, not only directing all his work to Him and for Him, but saying the psalms and portions of scripture that he knew by heart to himself as he worked at other jobs. The scheme sounds simple enough—it is one that we can practise ourselves—until Cassian links it up with the spirit of anger. The man in a rage cannot pray; contemplation is the still pool reflecting the sky, not the lake ruffled by the wind, or, to use Cassian's image, wrath blinds the eyes of the soul to the light of the sun of righteousness. We lose our tempers easily enough and forget

THE WISDOM OF THE DESERT

Cassian's striking juxtaposition of the Apostle's command to pray without ceasing with Christ's that we are not to come bringing our gift to the altar if we have a quarrel with our brother, but to go and make peace with him first. So that, if we go about nursing anger in our hearts, we fail in one command or the other, either we do not pray without ceasing or else offer to God not a prayer but "an obstinate temper with a rebellious spirit."

The same article about anger brings up the problem of the man who fled to the desert because he could not put up with other men. The desert, however, is only for those who are well on the way to perfection; solitude will help prayer, but equally it is fertile soil for the further growth of the faults and failings that we have still to get rid of. Cassian points out ironically enough that though the hermit may have no other man around to vent his temper on, he can still display it on inanimate objects like his knife or his pen!

Perhaps the stories about the temptations of Anthony, about wonders and miracles, have blinded us to the reality that was life in the desert, both for the monk living in a community and for the solitary. Excitements were few and far between; life was mostly a boring round of work and vigil and fast. There was virtually no variety, and their prayer even would be, as for everyone, largely a matter of steady hard work in the attempt to keep close to God. So then, accidie, the feeling that nothing is worth while and that the present life is useless and pointless, was particularly the temptation of the desert. The monk felt impelled to leave whatever he might be doing and go in search of some work that looked more useful and purposeful. To a certain extent he could counter the feeling by keeping hard at work, but, for the most part, the temptation had to be faced as such. The desert monks thought of themselves as soldiers of Christ, and it is the common experience of soldiers that most of their active service is made up of boredom and inaction. Battles are rare.

But it is not only in the desert that this sense of dejection and sloth and depression may seize upon one. The dog in the fable dropped the bone he had in his mouth in order to grip its juicy reflection. The temptation to go and immerse ourselves in a turmoil of various activities instead of holding fast to one thing, is of all times and for all men.

Pride and vainglory that come at the end of the list are the most dangerous of the whole group. For one thing, it is impossible ever to be free from the danger of falling into them. It is possible that the man who could not be overcome in a direct attack of some other temptation will then fall through the very extent of his conquest. The Christian life is based on the rock of humility, under men's feet undoubtedly, but firm and immovable ; the creature must realise that he is a creature and that all he is and has comes from God. Pride reverses this basic truth, and is an ever-present temptation ; it is possible to be proud of one's humility as if it was something that one had made for oneself.

Pride, however, can sometimes be useful, as one of Cassian's desert friends explained. Abbot Serapion discussed these eight principal faults when Cassian visited him, and said that pride could sometimes help a beginner by keeping him from falling into the other sins because he was afraid of the shame and disgrace that would follow. He told an amusing story of one effect of pride. In the monasteries of Syria there were men who could fast for five days together, going without food altogether. But when they went off into the desert to live as solitaries, keeping the normal daily fast until evening became an almost impossible task. A certain Abbot Macarius told one of these monks the reason for this sudden change in his powers of endurance :—"Here there is nobody to see you fast, and feed and support you with his praise of you ; but there you grew fat on the notice of others and the food of vainglory."

Abbot Serapion used a rather pleasant scriptural symbolism in talking about the eight faults and the way in which they can be got rid of— he compared them to the historical conquest of the Promised Land by the Israelites. In this metaphor, Egypt, which they left behind them, stood for gluttony, and the seven nations which they dispossessed for the remaining seven vices. Just so, said he, as the Israelites moved into the conquered lands, so as each vice is rooted out in us, the opposite virtue will move in and take possession.

One group of anchorites that Cassian visited lived in some old hilltop towns near the mouth of the Nile, a place where rich lands had been inundated and ruined by the sea, so that their original owners had deserted the district altogether. One of the hermits of the area, Abbot Nesteros, spoke to Cassian about the interpretation of the scriptures. To us, the elaborate symbolism that Abbot Serapion worked out about the eight faults and the Israelites seems at first strange and perhaps rather silly. It would be against Christian tradition to take this attitude, which has always seen in the historical events of the Bible, deeper spiritual meanings and symbols. Abbot Nesteros said that we would not understand or penetrate these spiritual meanings until we rid our-selves of sin and are really seeking perfection. Cassion brought up the problem that troubled so many scholars of the time who became

Christian, how could he get rid of the flood of pagan images derived from pagan literature, that filled his mind : to be told rather sharply that the problem would be solved if he applied the same eagerness to the Christian writings that he did to the pagan ones. Cassian's friend, Germanus, who journeyed with him through the desert, tried to argue with Nesteros over his statement that only the good man can really understand the marrow of scripture, pointing out that there had been many good scholars who were also wicked men. Nesteros countered with a distinction between the scholar as such with his book learning, and the saint who can really penetrate to the heart of scripture, enlightened by the Holy Ghost. This idea of a link between sanctity and real understanding of particular problems like the interpretation of scripture, is something real. The man in touch with God who is Truth itself is, other things being equal, more likely to be able to deal with particular truths and their relation one to another than the man who is out of contact with God and whose own interior life is a maze of confusion and conflict. Or, to go back to the mountain symbol, the climber who ascends the mountain of the Lord, looks back and sees all the country below spread out in its proper relationships : he sees the world like a map, whilst the traveller in the valley sees it in bits and pieces, first this house, then this cross-road and so on, and fails to grasp the pattern of the whole.

Abbot Moses, who lived in the desert of Scete, spoke to Cassian and Germanus at length about how we can arrive at this essential purity of heart, without which we cannot arrive at the kingdom of heaven. If he stressed that contemplation of God is the greatest good, Abbot Moses seems to have also been acutely aware of the problems of everyday life and of social injustice, for, in pointing out that in heaven we shall all be engaged in the contemplation of God in purity of heart and that there will then be no further need for works of practical charity and mercy, he spoke of present conditions :—"For what you call works of religion and mercy are needful in this life while these inequalities and differences of conditions still prevail ; but even here we should not look for them to be performed, unless such a large proportion of poor, needy, and sick folk abounded, which is brought about by the wickedness of men, viz., of those who have grasped and kept for their own use (without, however, using them) those things which were granted to all by the Creator of all alike."

Indeed the desert monks did not forget the rest of the world in the solitudes of the wilderness. Anthony went back to the city to help the persecuted ; the proceeds of the work done by the Egyptian monks which exceeded their own small needs were applied to works of mercy, for the relief of areas affected by famine and for the assistance of those in prison. The desert isolation helped the hermit to pray and get closer to God, but it did not separate him from his fellow men. In fact, Abbot Chaeremon, who lived like Nesteros in one of the deserted hilltop towns on the Nile mouth, explained to Cassian that the sign of a soul that is really reaching perfection is its intense sorrow for the sins of others.

Chaeremon told Cassian that there were three things that could bring a man to control and check his faults : fear of the law or of hell, hope of heaven, and the desire of goodness itself, three motives corresponding in graded sequence to the virtues of faith, hope and charity. Fear and hope ought to be the stages leading up to the highest motive, charity, so that we should come to love God "for the sake of nothing but His own love alone," just as God's love for us is entirely disinterested. A man who reaches this stage gets to have a great horror of sin for no other reason than his love for God, and so he comes to be able to pray for his persecutors and sorrow for their sins, becoming himself like God, "for in what can a weak and fragile human nature be like Him, except in always showing a calm love in its heart toward the good and evil, the just and unjust, in imitation of God, and by doing good for the love of goodness itself, arriving at that true adoption of the sons of God."

From these considerations, the desert conferences went on to consider the problem of evil which vexes many people today to such an extent. If God is good, why should evil be allowed to exist ? Talking to a certain Abbot Theodore, Cassian went into this question, beginning by asking why God had allowed a number of desert monks to be massacred by an invasion of robber bands. The incident had had the rather picturesque sequel of a fight over the bodies of the martyrs by the local people, one party claiming the relics because they came from the vicinity of the monks' settlement, the other struggling for possession on the ground that they had a better right because they belonged to the country where the monks had been born!

The key to the problem is, of course, the providence of God, that He is really in control of the whole world, that even the devils have no power of their own and can only do what is permitted them, and that out of the struggle and conflict good can and will be brought. Theodore told them that evil would never be forced upon a saint, in fact in a case like the recent massacre, the monks by becoming martyrs had gained greater glory. In the final analysis, an evil will not be "what he thinks, who brought them upon us in his rage and fury, but what *he* makes of them who endures them." But this does not justify the bad man's action, it remains a bad thing to kill a saint. Yet God can bring good out of the evil; Judas contributed to the salvation of men, but damned himself by his treachery.

It is not possible here to do more than indicate a few of the topics that were studied and discussed by the desert hermits and monks. But perhaps enough has been said to indicate that they were far from being solitary dreamers living in a world remote from reality. Of themselves, like the rest of us, they came good, bad and indifferent; the literature about the desert is full of references to bad monks and hermits who did not live up to their vocation. Their achievement was the working out of the monastic idea and its implications, and their ideas were to spread rapidly to the ends of the known world. Christian Celtic Ireland and Scotland cannot be understood without reference to the desert and its theology—the Bantry pillar does right in setting the praying figure beside St. Anthony and St. Paul and linking up their inspiration by a cross.

Further, the desert literature is full of delightful little stories, some of which have echoes in Irish traditions of the saints. There are odd little pieces of local colour. Cassian in his interview with Abbot Serenus, for instance, describes how thieves working at night used to identify valuables by scattering sand and listening to the different sounds it made as it fell on different objects. This extraordinary method of analysis was then compared to that of the devils, who scatter "the sand of evil suggestions" and watch the results so as to find out the weak point of a man which they can then attack in force.

There are stories of hermits who had nicknames, bynames as the Scottish Highlands would say. Thus Paphnutius, who lived in the desert of Scete, five miles from the nearest church, was called the Buffalo because of his great love of solitude. This hermit, even in extreme old age, used to walk the five miles each Saturday or Sunday to attend at the church and used to carry back with him his week's supply of water, as there was no spring available nearer to his hermitage.

Another hermit, faced with high transport costs, our modern problem, found that nothing would be gained by sending the palm leaf baskets that he used to make to the distant market. Still, he could not spend his time in idleness, so he made the baskets and then burned the pile at the end of the year!

But perhaps the most fascinating sidelight on the desert are the animal stories, which occur scattered through the literature. Not only the crow that brought St. Paul his bread, or the two lions that dug the same hermit's grave when St. Anthony came to bury his friend and had no means to do the work himself, but a whole series of incidents, which, even if in the realm of fable rather than of fact, do indicate the way in which the renunciation of the desert did not cut men off from creatures but brought them closer to them, and made the hyæna bring its blind pup to the hermit to have its eyes opened. The end of that particular story was the grateful hyæna returning the next day with the present of a fleece for the hermit! These animal stories were to be continued in the Irish stories of Irish saints and the tradition would live on with those about St. Francis. Contact with God brings about a new and purified love and sense of reverence for all the creatures that He has made, and the animals seem to sense and respond to it. The white pony of Iona wept upon the dying Columcille's shoulder, and the same saint befriended the storm-spent crane that landed on the island.

According to St. John Chrysostom, Cassian's friend, there is yet another way of thinking about the desert, this time as a symbol for each of us. Commenting on St. Matthew's account of Christ's temptation in the desert, St. Chrysostom says that not only Christ but all God's children will be led into the desert by the Holy Ghost. This is because it is not enough for them to be idle, the Holy Spirit urges them on to do something great for God, and this endeavour puts them out in the desert from the point of view of the devil because there is no unrighteousness, in which the devil delights, in this "desert" of good work and effort. We must now trace out how the quiet contemplation of the historic desert came to spill over into the violence of apostolic action, as the quiet spring upon the mountain ridge flows over the cliff edge and thunders down to the valley in a cataract.

Chapter Four

THE FIRE ON THE HILL

THREE times the risen Christ asked St. Peter if he loved Him, and in answer to each of the saint's affirmations gave the command to go and feed His sheep. The command was not given to Peter alone, the love of God is not something to be selfishly hugged to oneself, but something that drives a man forth to teach all nations. So then the symbols of Christianity are the city set on the hilltop; the light of Christ, the sun of righteousness; the Easter fire that St. Patrick lit upon the ridge of Slane, the sudden blaze that challenged an Ireland waiting in darkness for its own pagan fire festival. And this was the hallmark of the faith of the Celtic saints, this urge based upon a life of prayer and penance, to travel the world and bring it knowledge of truth and of the Son of the Virgin.

Christ Himself in His own life had already marked out the trail, His forty days fast in the desert, the life of pure contemplation, leading on to His work of preaching and teaching. The text books tend to draw too sharp a line between the life of action and of pure contemplation; in reality the two intermingle. For, although the active life prepares for that of pure prayer and union with God, as St. Gregory the Great put it, training first in the camp of action before going on to hold the fortress of contemplation; the fullness of contemplation spills over into a much more effective and efficient form of activity, the work of the apostle who lives and moves in close contact and union with God. The Christian's objective is to imitate and follow Christ, to share in His love for men, the same love that brought Him to the cross.

The story of St. Martin of Tours forms the link between the desert ideals of solitude and uninterrupted contemplation of God, and the ideal of the monk who is also an apostle and preacher—the ideal of the Celtic Church.

The fame of the eastern deserts and their monks and hermits spread rapidly over Europe, and seems to have been known to the youthful Martin. He was born about the year 330 in the town of Sabaria in what is now Hungary and, although his parents were pagans, was completely fascinated by Christ and wanted to become a Christian and go and live in the desert. His father, who was a Military Tribune, had quite other ideas and when the boy reached the age of fifteen and became liable for conscription to the army, reported him to the authorities, who forcibly enrolled him in the Roman forces.

In the army, Martin, although still not baptised, lived like a monk and a Christian, keeping only one servant with whom he used to take turn about, each waiting on the other. At the age of twenty-two, he received the sacrament of baptism, but did not immediately leave the army because his tribune begged him to stay on so that the two of them could leave together and both abandon the world. When Martin did leave, he at once began to follow out his ideal, and sought out St. Hilary, the bishop of Poitiers, with whom he spent some time, before going to visit his parents and trying to convert them, a project which only succeeded in the case of his mother.

A Middle-Irish homily on St. Martin, probably written in the 13th century, rather pleasantly sums up the change that had come about in Martin's life when he gave up the career of Roman soldier for that of a monk, a soldier of Christ :—

> "Now a multitude of the saints and the righteous of the Lord, both in the Old and the New Testament, cast from them service and warfare on behalf of the Devil and World and worldly wealth for service of the heavenly king, to wit, God. For no one could serve them both : even as he cast from him the earthly warfare for the heavenly warfare, to wit, the high saint, noble, venerable, . . . holy Martin, high bishop of Tours."

Eventually Martin rejoined St. Hilary and about 360, founded a monastery near Poitiers at Liguge. It seems to have been a group of hermits gathered around Martin, just as hermits had gathered round Anthony in the desert. Martin's fame spread, and although his wish was to remain in the quiet of his cell, the citizens of Tours managed to compel him to become their bishop.

Martin the bishop continued to live as Martin the monk. To escape continual interruption from visitors, he established another monastic group about two miles from his cathedral, on a plot of ground between the mountain side and a bend of the River Loire. Here he and the monks lived either in wooden huts on the flat or rock shelters on the hillside. The older men seem to have been entirely occupied in prayer, but the younger ones did some copying work in addition ; they seem to have met only for prayer at the church. But though the group sounds very like that of Anthony in the desert, there is a new element entering in. The desert monks and hermits were normally not priests and they wished above everything to avoid holding office in the world beyond the desert. Martin too had had orders forced on him, almost, protesting his unworthiness, and Martin's monks at Marmoutier outside Tours would have the same attitude, yet they did not in the end refuse and numbers later became bishops. For, as Martin's friend and biographer, Sulpicius Severus wrote "what city or church was there which did not covet a priest from the monastery of Martin ?" The contemplation of the desert was beginning to lead to action in the world around it.

Martin himself is generally regarded as both the father of western monasticism (although the spread of monasticism over Europe was a gradual affair, involving many other founders as well) and as the apostle of Gaul. As bishop of Tours, he set out on missionary journeys across the surrounding country, preaching, converting the pagan populations and destroying their heathen temples. He was not a highly educated man, but his friend, Sulpicius, says that in spite of that he spoke faultless Latin. He had a very considerable charm of manner and a rather amusing way of pointing the moral from unexpected examples, if Sulpicius reports him correctly. Thus he once pointed out a shorn sheep as an example of the Gospel precept, which the sheep had fulfilled, having had two coats it had given one to another who had none! Sulpicius says too that he was always occupied in prayer or reading, and at no time did his mind ever cease from prayer. And further, that "so great was his patience towards those who injured him, that, although he was chief priest, even clerks of the lowest orders might wrong him without his ever removing them from their position, or even, as far as in him lay, from his affection."

This man, whom the Martyrology of Oengus the Culdee (c. 800) describes as "the mount of gold of the western world," was to be one of the chief inspirations of Celtic monasticism. The principal link seems to have been through St. Ninian, though there were many other subsidiary channels as well. Ninian was a Romanized Briton from the south of Scotland. His dates are thought to be from c. 362 to c. 432. It was then still possible to move freely about the area of the now disintegrating Roman Empire, and young Ninian went south to Rome to complete his education. Coming back, he visited Martin and, like everyone else, fell under his spell. After he left Martin and returned to Scotland, Ninian's great foundation at Whithorn, Candida Casa, the White Church, in Galloway, was dedicated to Martin, news of whose death in 397 reached Scotland as the little church was being built. The monastery round it was planned to resemble that of Marmoutier, but it was meant from the very start not merely as a place of solitude and contemplation, but also a springboard for action. According to tradition, Ninian was consecrated a bishop by the Pope and came back with a definite mandate for the evangelisation of the country we now call Scotland. Martin had had to be pried out of his hermit's cell, Ninian from the very first set out to combine the life of contemplation with that of preaching and travelling about the country. He and his monks went far, right up the east coast of Scotland, leaving a trail of churches at sites which still today bear Ninian's name. Galloway too looks across the narrow channel to Ireland, and Candida Casa's fame soon spread across the sea ; Irishmen came to study there, to work in Scotland before returning to Ireland, and Scotsmen went from Galloway to Ireland. There were other routes by which monasticism came into Ireland : through the southern ports and by St. Patrick's teaching and organisation, but Candida Casa seems to have been a principal source of inspiration. Tradition says that St. Enda, who is thought of as the founder of the first great Irish monastery, on the islands of Aran in Galway Bay, was trained at Whithorn.

Knowledge of Christianity filtered slowly into Ireland, and there were already a number of Christians and saints, more especially in the south of the country, before St. Patrick mounted his great mission in 432. Yet to Patrick, the Irish owed the first systematic and country-wide preaching and organising of the Faith, and he is rightly thought of as the apostle of the Irish. St. Patrick, however, represents a quite different line of approach to God from that of Martin and Ninian, and in his lack of book learning—which he mentions in his writings—is well away from the regular line of development of Irish Celtic saints.

Martin and Ninian were men who from the very first had turned to God, who had never known a time when they did not love Him and desire Him more than anything else. Patrick was a nominal Christian, whose vocation had almost to be forced upon him against his own will. The hermit Paphnutius, he who was nicknamed the Buffalo, told Cassian that there were three sorts of vocation, direct from God, or through the example of the saints, or by compulsion—such as the loss of one's goods and the like misfortune. Patrick belongs to the third group. Carried off to Ireland as a slave by Irish raiders, he only began to turn to God in the solitude and loneliness of the hillside where he herded his master's swine. Even after he escaped from Ireland, he seems to have had no intention of going back to convert the men who had injured him, until the idea of so doing was brought home to him by a vivid dream in which the voice of the Irish asked him to come back to them. By these devious paths did the British Patrick come to Ireland, and to the lighting of the Easter fire on Slane hill. The spring of the year following the autumn of Patrick's arrival, Easter coincided with the Celtic spring fire festival, the time when all the fires were put out, and then relit from a new ceremonial bonfire. The traditional account tells how Patrick broke this curfew in lighting his Easter fire, and how after conflict with the druids who tried to get him to put it out, he got the necessary permission from the High King of Ireland to set about his work of preaching.

Whether the tradition is true is another matter; it has been suggested that in point of fact the Church got the idea of the Easter ceremony of the new fire from Celtic sources, where the symbolism of fire was particularly well known and understood. But true or not, the fire on the hill is symbolic of Irish Celtic Christian activity, of a torch held up to the world, of a dogged refusal to give in to either force or argument to put it out, and of a consuming fire of the love of God that would not let a man rest but must drive him continually on to fresh effort and activity.

For Celtic Christianity was nearly entirely monastic in organisation, but it was not a monasticism in the sense of the desert monks, but of the monasticism that Martin's had been forced to become and that Ninian's had been from the beginning. The monk was deeply involved in apostolic activity; he used his monastery as a base from which to travel Ireland, and to adventure across the seas to Europe and to the British islands. It was a foreshadowing of the Dominican and Franciscan vocations of later centuries. It developed into a massive missionary movement, beginning in the 6th century, when St. Columcille in 563 and St. Moluag in 562 went across to western Scotland, and St. Columbanus in 590, set out for Europe. From then on, Irish missionaries and scholars poured in a steady stream over Europe's roads and waterways, founding monasteries, teaching, reforming, and spreading Irish culture and ideas.

The monastic basis of the Celtic Church was probably largely determined by the existing organisation of the country itself. Ireland had no towns, its population was exclusively rural and lived scattered amongst the fields and pastures. The larger landowners lived each in his self-supporting rath, or fortified homestead, with a complete staff to do all necessary work on the spot; the Celtic monastery was this secular grouping carried over into the Church. The early Celtic monasteries are very much like the early Celtic fortified homesteads, the circling wall, the small rough huts inside, with, in the case of the monasteries, the addition of a church or churches. The country of Ireland was divided up into a number of small states called *tuatha*, these were grouped into the seven great divisions of Ireland, and these in turn came under the rule of the High King of the whole country; the organisation of the Celtic Church was linked with this civil arrangement, for Patrick's method was to get the interest and assistance of each small chieftain who would give the Celtic clergy land for a foundation, sometimes an old rath that could be adapted into a new monastic settlement. St. Columbanus, working among the new states that were coming into being in Europe followed out the same plan, of making his first contact with the local king. In Ireland, the scheme meant that there was a close link between the local lord, the tuath's principal monastery and the people; there was a clannishness about the scheme that sometimes, but not always, resulted in the abbots being chosen from particular families and the monastery's fortunes being tied up with those of the particular division of Ireland in which it lay. In Scotland, something similar happened, there being a division between the Picts of the eastern part of the country and the intrusive Irish settlers of the west Highlands, amongst whom St. Columcille worked both in the religious and political fields.

The country to which Patrick and Ninian preached was not, however, an uncultured civilisation because it was an agricultural one. The standard of housing was very poor, but against that rather bleak background flourished all the glory of Celtic art, and learning of all kinds was held in high esteem. This had its effect on the formation of the Celtic monks. In the desert, and with St. Martin too, the stress had fallen on prayer and on manual labour, rather than on purely intellectual pursuits. The hermit, who like St. Jerome, took his books with him into the desert was rare, and Jerome's own hermit adventure was not very long lived. St. Basil, indeed, who was the great inspiration of the eastern monks, had laid stress upon study, but, in general, there is the contrast between the desert monk or hermit, praying and plaiting mats of palm leaves or cultivating a little plot of ground, and the saint like Augustine, who combined the life of prayer with his work as bishop and author and linked it up with the philosophical knowledge and training of his pagan days. The Irish monk joined the two traditions, the student and the farmer, the man equally at home with a philosophical problem and a curragh. Irish hagiography is full of stories of the boyhood of the Celtic saints, in which they are described herding cattle on the hillside and studying their books at the same time. The ideal set forth by the ancient Rule of St. Ailbe of Emly (c. 700-950) is to be wise, learned and pious.

The period of the Celtic Church extended from the time of Ninian and Patrick to St. Malachy's reform and introduction of the Cistercian Order to Ireland in the 12th century. The period had its ups and downs, quarrels between the different divisions of Ireland, the invasion of the Norsemen and the Danes, and the inevitable slackening off of fervour that overtakes all people after a time, followed by reaction in the shape of a reform movement. Yet over all this period, looking at the material available from Ireland, and in much lesser amount from Scotland, it is possible to recognize something, a certain flash of spirit and interpretation that is essentially of the Celtic Church, its habit of mind and particular way of looking at things. The Celtic saints came as different as do modern Irish and Scots men, yet about the whole series there is this distinctive character, just as there is a distinctive flavour to be found common to modern Celts. We can then set about studying this angle upon life that is at once Celtic and Catholic.

The sources for such a study are not in the "Lives" of the Irish saints, which are built up too largely of miracles and wonders and the Irish love of a good story to be of much help. Rather, we must turn to the books that the Celtic monks used and studied, the scriptures, the Fathers of the Church, and, in addition, since they felt no bias against the paganism of the Mediterranean countries because it was different from their own, the classics, whose beguiling charm had given so much concern to men like St. Jerome. With the Latin classics and history, they also studied their own existing body of tradition, saga and history. Pre-Christian Ireland already had a great tradition of poetry, and some of her saints like Columcille received part of their training in the bardic schools which continued to flourish.

The second source of information about the outlook of the Celtic saints comes from the remaining fragments of Celtic liturgy, prayer and commentary that have survived, first of all the Viking attacks, then the

Anglo-Norman invasions, and finally the Reformation. This material includes the so-called Antiphonary of Bangor, which was taken to Europe for safe keeping from the Viking attacks and which belongs to the 7th century, and the Stowe Missal which is connected with the Culdee or Céili Dé reform movement of the late 8th and early 9th centuries. From this same period of reform also seem to come the various "Rules" of the Celtic saints. These "Rules," which really consist of collections of maxims on various topics, seem to have been given the name of earlier saints who founded or were in some other way connected with the monastery in which the "Rule" eventually came to be composed.

So far as the surviving material is representative, Irish learning was mainly concerned with conservation and study of existing material rather than with new and original thought. The work of the brilliant, if erroneous, Johannes Scotus Eriugena, one of the great scholars of 9th century Europe, must be excepted : there may have been others like him whose work has perished, but, in general, the time was not ripe nor the material fully available, for the kind of synthesis and original thought that was to be developed later in the Middle Ages.

The third source of information about the mind of the Celtic saints is to be found in Celtic art, in metalwork like the Ardagh chalice and in stone carving like the High Crosses. And finally, we can get further information about the sort of men they were by tracking after them, and looking at the places they chose to settle in, places that nearly always combine natural advantages in the way of land for farming and water supply and connection with communication lines, with great natural beauty. Fully to understand the Celtic saints, it is necessary to understand the feel of a boat as she lifts over a breaking swell, or to crouch in the cold of the dawn by the ruined hilltop oratory and watch the sun come up out of the mist.

Chapter Five

THE CELTIC BREASTPLATE

DAWN strikes the high places first, the valleys deep in shade; the sudden flash of the sun on the mountain tops changing the snowfields of the corries from grey to rose-pink. The sea lies dull, till the light catches it, setting each wave etched and sharp, building a brilliant pathway to the east. Long before the light comes, the birds have word of it in the woods, a stirring in the branches, a sudden call, then one by one, the full-throated chorus of the dawn. The sun lifts higher and shines into the dew-drenched glens, where the wild roses edge the road-sides. The most disillusioned remark I ever heard was that of a man who said he had seen too many dawns to want to see another, for the coming of the light is the creation story over again, a daily mystery and miracle. The darkness that comes at the end of the evening is so embracing and final a thing that you would think it would never grow light again, until there comes that first faint lighting of the sky long before sunrise. Because the sun has always risen in the past is still no guarantee for the future, either for ourselves, for we may never live to see another dawn, or for the world, for the morrow might be the Day of Judgment.

It is our disillusioned world that takes these things for granted, whilst the child and the poet and the Celt snatch greedily at the awful transitoriness of created beauty, feeling the heartbreak in the blue of the sky, in the shimmer of sunshine on birch leaves, in the rainbow caught in the driven spray of the waves; a perfection of loveliness that slips through the fingers like a melody heard distantly across a lake on a summer evening.

It is against this background that I would set the Celtic form of prayer called "lorica" or breastplate, a prayer which stands out as perhaps the most characteristic of the private prayers of the Celtic

45

Church. That of Patrick, which is the best known to most people, has about it an air of just such a setting. Its challenging phrases ring out against the first light of dawn, against the fang of Skellig Rock, on whose summit the beehive cells and oratories of the Celtic 6th century hermitage still stand intact. The rock and the water, the low sun lighting the hills of Kerry and throwing the fantastic shadow of the Skellig Rock onto the glittering sea, the white birds wheeling over the smaller neighbour rock of Little Skellig, the salt on the tongue and the wind rustling amongst the broken rocks : this is the moment to be coming out of those beehive huts plastered on the island height and to be climbing to the ledge above them and flinging St. Patrick's Breastplate like a challenge into the wind.

> "I arise today,
>> might of Heaven
>> brightness of sun
>> whiteness of snow
>> splendour of fire
>> speed of light
>> swiftness of wind
>> depth of sea
>> stability of earth
>> firmness of rock!"

The lorica prayer rears itself up from the surviving collection of Celtic prayers and hymns just as the Skellig of St. Michael springs from the sea off the coast of Kerry, a challenge to our complacent attitude of disbelief in angels and devils and the whole existence of unseen but real spiritual beings. The lorica is the temptation of St. Anthony and the teaching of the desert fathers put in a jewelled setting of poetry and music. Just as Celtic craftsmen made the glory of the Cross of Cong to enshrine a relic of the True Cross, so Celtic genius made the lorica prayers to weave a glittering commentary around the victory of Christ crucified over the devil and the fallen angels, over the powers of evil.

For Celtic Christianity believed in the reality of the demons ; that they could haunt the rocks of Skellig just as the gannets do, even if you could not see them as you could the birds. And between these invisible foes and yourself was the cross of Christ, the sign of victory, the standard of the host of heaven. In pagan times, Celtic Ireland had had a rhythmic spell formula, which was supposed to produce invisibility ; the Celtic Church took this old verse form and turned it into a new Christian prayer, a prayer which would protect one against evil of all kinds, making the man who recited it to all intents and purposes invisible to the demons.

So the monk on Skellig Rock could, in the cold bright light of sunrise, put on the armour of God, invoke St. Michael, the patron of the hermitage, to help him with all the angel armies of heaven, and draw round him, as the hero in the sagas flung over his shoulders the cloak of invisibility, the awful power of the Trinity.

"I arise today,

> Might of God for my piloting
> Wisdom of God for my guidance
> Eye of God for my foresight
> Ear of God for my hearing
> Word of God for my utterance
> Hand of God for my guardianship
> Path of God for my precedence
> Shield of God for my protection
> Host of God for my salvation,

against snares of demons
against allurements of vices
against solicitations of nature
against every person that wishes me ill far and near
alone and in a crowd."

Christ is king, this is the message of the lorica prayers and their source of power, the cross stands for victory and the Christian can share the Victor's spoils. "If anybody doubts the power of the Cross," said St. Cyril of Jerusalem, preaching to the candidates for baptism in the Lent of 347 or 348, "let him enquire of the devils." Cassian notes how the intensity of the devilish attacks on the monks of the desert had slackened off as more and more monks settled there, but wondered, rather cynically, whether it was so much due to their conquest by the Cross, as to the loss of fervour by the latter day monks and hermits, making them less worth the devil's time to bother with! But for the Celtic saints, the sign of the cross was to be made constantly, to sain every activity, and drive out the lurking demons, helter-skelter, before it. The Lorica of Mugron (comarb (successor in the line of abbots in the Columban monastic group) of Columcille, died 980) signs the cross upon every part of the body, eyes, cheeks, ears, mouth, back, side, shoulders, hands and so on, and then sets it, like a rainbow in the sky over the whole world and over every activity.

"The Cross of Christ with me in my good luck, in my bad luck;
The Cross of Christ against every strife, abroad or at home;
The Cross of Christ in the East with courage, the Cross of Christ
    in the West at sunset;
South, North without any stay, the Cross of Christ without any
    delay;
The Cross of Christ above toward the clear sky, the Cross of
    Christ below towards earth.
There shall come no evil nor suffering to my body or to my soul,
The Cross of Christ at my sitting, the Cross of Christ at my lying;
The Cross of Christ all my strength, till we reach the King of
    Heaven!"

St. Cyril carefully instructed his catechumens, telling them of the
many opposing forces that the Christian had to meet and overcome.
They were, in baptism, going to receive their armour against all these
different attackers, heresies, Jews, Samaritans, Gentiles, against whom
the Christian required a whole battery of different darts to hurl at them.
Patrick's lorica carried on the idea, listing the things that we need to
struggle against.

"I invoke therefore all these forces to intervene between me
    and every fierce merciless force that may come upon my body and
        my soul:
    against incantations of false prophets
    against black laws of paganism
    against false laws of heresy
    against deceit of idolatry
    against spells of women and smiths and druids
    against all knowledge that is forbidden the human soul."

St. Patrick's Lorica is at least as old as the 8th century, it seems to
be older, though there is no evidence that Patrick wrote it himself, and
there is an archaic ring about the prayer for protection against the spells
of women and smiths and druids; it is of the very stuff of a young
Church establishing itself in a pagan countryside. Yet if we no longer
fear spells, can we so easily write off the other evils which are of all
time? It seems that we are inclined to see only half the world, whilst
the Celtic saints saw it whole, built of spiritual and material things and,
reaching out for the sword of the spirit, joined in the battle. The change
that has come over us is almost symbolised by the rationalist and
materialist twist that occurs in the refrain of that favourite Protestant
hymn, which reads "Onward, Christian soldiers, Marching *as to* war,"

thus reducing the huge and heroic battle of St. Paul, "against principalities and powers, against the rulers of the world of this darkness, against the spirits of wickedness in the high places," to the make-believe level of army manoeuvres.

This is not Christian doctrine, the battle is not a mere symbol or a make-believe exercise. The Christian does become the soldier of Christ the King when he is confirmed, and he is intended to arm himself with spiritual weapons for the only war whose issue really matters. It is the violent who will fight their way into heaven, but they will not be fighting alone : the Christian is not a free-lance cavalier, he is backed by the power of the Trinity by the merits of Christ's life on earth, and his companions in arms are the angels and the saints. The first three verses of St. Patrick's Lorica set forth the line of battle.

"I arise today :
        vast might, invocation of the Trinity,—
        belief in a Threeness,
        confession of Oneness,
        meeting in the Creator.
    I arise today :
        the might of Christ's birth and His baptism,
        the might of His Crucifixion and Burial,
        the might of His Resurrection and Ascension,
        the might of His Descent to the judgment of Doom.
    I arise today :
        might of grades of Cherubim,
        in obedience of Angels,
        in ministrations of Archangels,
        in hope of resurrection for the sake of reward,
        in prayers of Patriarchs,
        in prophecies of Prophets,
        in preachings of Apostles,
        in faiths of Confessors,
        in innocence of Holy Virgins,
        in deeds of righteous men."

The lorica could become much more specific in its invocations and therefore much more like the ordinary litanies with which we are familiar. Thus a lorica-like prayer, dated c. 800-850 and ascribed to a certain Colmán moccu Cluasaig who was a lector in Cork, who is said to have composed it for protection against the yellow plague, invokes

the help of a whole series of individuals ranging from the Old Testament
to some of the Irish saints. It begins in the typical lorica strain :—

"God's blessing lead us, help us! May Mary's Son cover us!
May we be under His safeguard to-night! Whither we go may be
He guard us well!

Whether in rest or in motion, whether sitting or standing,
the Lord of Heaven against every strife, this is the prayer that we
will pray."

It then becomes a litany of invocations :—

"Noah and Abraham, Isaac the wonderful son,
may they surround us against pestilence, that famine may not come
to us!"

Ireland, because of her pre-Christian standards of learning, had two
languages of equal value for study and in use amongst her learned men,
Irish and Latin. Latin was the language of the official liturgy but Irish
was often used in private prayers and hymns as well as in various works
of scholarship. So familiar were the Irish with the two languages that
they developed a rather attractive habit of switching from one to the
other in the same work, and Colmán's hymn, written mainly in Irish,
shows this trait well.

"John the Baptist we invoke, may he be a safeguard to us, a protection!
may Jesus with His apostles be for our help against danger!

May Mary and Joseph herd us et spiritus Stephani
from every strait may be the commemoration of Ignatius' name
release us!

May every martyr, every hermit, every saint that has been in chastity,
be a shield to us for our protection, be a dart from us against the
devils!

The Latin might form the rhyme at the end of the couplet :—

"Melchisedech rex Salem incerto de semine
may his prayers deliver us ab omni formidine."

The angels are invoked to help us, as they had helped men before.

"As He sent the angel that loosed Peter from the chain,
may he be sent to us for our aid, may every unsmooth be smooth
before us!

Latin reacted upon Irish and gave it new loan words. The Latin, lorica, breastplate, passed into Irish in the form *lurech*, and this is the name given in Irish to the Lorica of Bishop Sanctan. Nothing is known about this Sanctan except that he is said to have been a Briton, his lorica prayer is 9th century in date. Its phrases have a pleasantly Celtic twist to them, and I quote three typical couplets :—

"May God help me—holy the invocation—against every danger
that I risk!
Let there be a bridge of life beneath me, the blessing of God the
Father above me.

Let not a hard cast, which maddens, which perturbs, come to me
apart from God's Son!
Christ protect me against every violent death, against fire, against
the tumult of the sea!

I will utter the praises of Mary's Son, who fights our white fights ;
Creative God will answer, a corslet (*lurech*) of which my tongue
boasteth."

The idea of the Christian as a soldier which runs through all the lorica prayers seems to have particularly caught the Irish fancy, taking colour it almost seems from the Fianna [Fingalian] hero companies. "Soldier of Christ," "Island soldier," these were the phrases used about men like Columcille and Moluag, running their boats ashore on Hebridean beaches, or of the continental campaign, the invasion of Europe, that was headed by Columbanus. The development of the idea, however, is part of the story of the Catholic Church as a whole and its origins go back to the Old Testament. In the Book of Job, man's life on earth is compared to warfare : " militia est vita hominis super terram" (Job. vii. 1). Then St. Paul took up the idea and developed it into something glittering and sparkling, a heroic battle and a hero's arms : the armour of God, girt with truth, justice for breastplate, the shield of faith, the helmet of salvation, the sword of the spirit. It outshone the brilliance of the descriptions of the heroes of Irish saga and history. The metaphor occurred again and again in the writings of the Fathers of the Church, which the Celtic Church knew and studied, and maybe the man on Skellig found St. Augustine's words about fighting down our bad habits by casting them out from the vantage point of the citadel of Christian warfare, singularly appropriate to that high, springing rock. And further, the Celtic Church had cause for a special liking for the concept of the soldier of Christ, because of her devotion to St. Martin of Tours, who had so very obviously never ceased to be a soldier but only changed his supreme commander and the objectives of his war.

The martyrs had, in the early Church, been considered the front line troops, the real soldiers of Christ. It is thus that they are singled out in the Te Deum: "Te Martyrum candidatus laudat exercitus" (The white-robed army of martyrs praises thee). Irish devotion to the Christian martyrs was very strong, and one of the most beautiful hymns in the Antiphonary of Bangor is in their honour. The Antiphonary, a collection of prayers and hymns compiled at Bangor in Ulster between the years 680 and 691, and apparently intended as a companion volume to the psalterium and lectionarium, represents the authentic voice of the early Celtic Church in Ireland. The hymn in honour of the martyrs included in this collection is not found in any other MS.; it seems probable that it was written in Ireland and it has been suggested that it may have been modelled on an earlier Greek hymn. It employs a unique verse form, with an irregular number of syllables in each line but a regular pattern in the recurrence of the accent, producing a strangely attractive measure. The idea of the martyrs as men who have fought and conquered and won the victor's crown runs through the whole composition, heaven re-echoing with their triumphant Alleluia. Its first verse outlines the whole concept:—

> "Sacratissimi martyres summi Dei,
> Bellatores fortissimi Christi regis,
> Potentissimi duces exercitus Dei,
> Victores in coelis Deo canentes,
>   Alleluia."

Yet the hymn ends with the petition that we too will reach the heavenly Jerusalem and join in the same chorus of praise. The man who died for the Faith was in the front line, but all Christians were in the fight. So St. Paul could write to Timothy and tell him to work as a good soldier of Jesus Christ. Later, for St. Basil (330-379), the monk has almost taken the special place of the martyr with the ending of persecution, but the war, against the world and the flesh and the devil, continues for all.

So then, the symbolism of the Christian soldier is remarkably rich and varied. It is the war of angel against devil, of the grace of God against temptations, of virtue against vice, of prayer against the power of the temporal world. The Christian's weapons are various, he must attack as well as defend. The saint's mind, in fact, in "this war of temptations, being at once defended by the shield of patience, and begirt with the swords of love, obtains resolution for the enduring of bad treatment, and puts forth kindness in the recompensing good, so as to both to receive stoutly the weapons of enmities, and return forcibly the darts of love. For he does not in any way go armed to the wars, who either taking a shield, uses no swords, or using swords is not protected by a shield. And hence the soldier of God, encountered by a war of adversity, ought both to hold before him the shield of patience, lest he perish, and being prompt to preach he should launch the darts of love, that he may win the victory."

That quotation is from a book well known in Ireland, St. Gregory the Great's immensely long but continuously interesting commentary on the Book of Job, *Moralia in Librum Job*. St. Gregory (died 604) used the text of the Book of Job as a jumping off ground for a complete series of reflections on the Christian life and on prayer ; the work became a kind of standard text on the subject and was very widely read. In Ireland, a shortened version was made by a certain Laid-cend (died 661), so that those who lacked the time or energy to plough through the whole bulk of the work could skim off the cream. With the Celtic lorica prayers in mind, we can read St. Gregory's warnings about the very various lines of attack on us by the devil, and how we may counter them. "Against a famine, they (holy men) have the sustenance of God's word ; against the sword of war, they have the shield of continency ; against the scourge of the tongue, the defence of patience ; against the hurt of outward misfortune, they have the aid of inward love. Hence in a marvellous manner it is brought to pass, that the more manifold the temptations which the craft of the enemy brings upon them, so much the richer in virtues are the wary soldiers of God rendered."

In fact, the mind of the lorica prayers is only that of the Catholic Church as a whole in a Celtic setting. St. Thomas Aquinas, in his prayer after Communion, asked that it would protect him with the armour of faith and the shield of a good will (Sit mihi armatura fidei, et scutum bonae voluntatis) and defend him against the wiles of his enemies, whether visible or invisible. In the *Summa Theologica* he brings up the problem of the assaults of the demons, which were so real to the Celtic saints and are so unreal to us, and asks the question, "Whether Men are assailed by the demons ?" (I. q. 114. a. 1), concluding that they can be and are. Yet to us now, the invisible foe is subconsciously disregarded, just as the invisible angels are thrust to the backs of our minds, not because either demon or angel is invisible, for so are the different components of the atom in which we all fervently believe, but because they cannot be scientifically recorded and because they are out of fashion. When the Preface of the Mass links up the Church on earth with the praises of the glittering host of heaven, we are inclined to let the words slip past as mere rhetoric and never see them as a simple statement of fact.

But the Celtic saints were intensely aware of this interpenetration of the material world by the spiritual. Catholic liturgy has always stressed the same fact : in exorcism and blessing the Church brings the power of the Cross to bear on material things, to drive out the lurking demon and hallow them for Christian use. If we have lost that sense of the presence of spiritual beings, we have lost the wholeness of our view of the world, turned our backs on a whole section of creation. If you accept belief in God and the Christian revelation, you must also accept belief in the creation of spiritual as well as material things ; in the angels, who like men, were given the freedom to choose God or reject Him. The malice and evil that prowls the world is not entirely the result of unruly human passions let loose by Adam's decision. The devil made his choice too, St. Peter in his first Epistle likens him to a roaring lion seeking someone to devour, and he is only too ready to pounce at any sign of weakness.

Ireland still retains this feeling of intimacy with the unseen world round us, and, in the remoter districts, the milker may yet sign the cross on the cow's flank with a finger dipped in the froth from the full pail. And it is worth setting this present-day Irish tradition against the actions of the Celtic monks, who sained everything they touched and used with the cross. St. Adamnan's account of St. Columcille on Iona and the demon in the milk pail is well known, but not to be passed over for all that as a mere fable.

The story, for Adamnan knew Iona intimately, carries with it the authentic flavour of the Hebrides, the glint of the sun on the sea, the short turf of the pasture, spangled with daisies, the red granite of the island of Mull across the Sound of Iona, the dusty white island paths. The cattle are out, so the story implies, on the summer pasture and, as is still Hebridean custom, had been milked in the open there. The lad who did the milking comes down the white sandy pathway, past the knoll on which Columcille's cell stands and pauses at the open door, to ask the saint's blessing on the full pail. Columcille looks up at the figure darkening the bright space of the doorway and makes the sign of the cross, whereupon the wooden lid flies off and half the milk is spilt on the ground. The alarmed milker fell on his knees, but Columcille told him to get up and bring him the pail, with the remaining milk in it to bless, explaining that the trouble arose from the boy's neglecting to sign the pail with the cross before putting the milk into it, and thus allowing a demon to continue lurking there. According to Adamnan, the blessing of Columcille was able to restore the full amount of milk, but whether or no one is willing to accept the idea of the saint's being able to do something about spilled milk, the gist of the story remains as an authentic account of a usual custom (signing each article before use with the cross) and of a deep seated belief in the reality of the invisible world.

Long ago, the Book of Wisdom (ch. V) had told how God would protect the just, that He would cover them with His right hand and defend them with His holy arm. "And his zeal will take armour, and he will arm the creature for the revenge of his enemies. He will put on justice as a breastplate, and will take true judgment instead of a helmet; he will take equity for an invincible shield." The Celtic Lorica carried on the same idea, the Christian circled by the power of God as the flame came down on the Apostles at Pentecost.

"Christ for my guardianship today
             against poison, against burning,
             against drowning, against wounding,
   that there may come to me a multitude of rewards:
   Christ with me, Christ before me,
   Christ behind me, Christ in me,
   Christ under me, Christ over me,
   Christ to right of me, Christ to left of me,
   Christ in lying down, Christ in sitting, Christ in rising up,
   Christ in the heart of every person, who may think of me!
   Christ in the mouth of everyone who may speak to me!
   Christ in every eye which may look on me!
   Christ in every ear, which may hear me!
                              (Lorica of St. Patrick).

Chapter Six

THE MASS AND THE LITURGY

THE Ardagh chalice, now preserved in the National Museum in Dublin, seems, in the glitter and perfection of its workmanship, to crystallise and bring down to earth all the romance of the legends of the Holy Grail. Of silver, set with crystal, garnet, amber, enamel and glass in restrained but almost miraculously delicate designs, the chalice is probably of eighth century date and the most precious European chalice that has survived from before the twelfth century.

Yet to look at the Ardagh chalice merely as one of the great achievements of Celtic artists in Ireland would be to miss the very point and purpose of its making, which was to be merely the setting for something infinitely more precious, for the wine of the Mass changed at the moment of consecration into the Blood of Christ. The Ardagh chalice is the symbol of the vivid belief of the Celtic Church in the Catholic dogma of transubstantiation, and a pointer to the source of the dynamic energy of the Celtic saints. The surviving fragments of Celtic liturgy leave us in no doubt about the nature of Celtic faith in the Mass. It is a faith perhaps best summed up in the *Sancti venite*, the ancient hymn in the Antiphonary of Bangor which was sung when the priests received communion. *The Sancti venite* is an Irish composition and is claimed as the oldest surviving Eucharistic hymn of Western Europe. It puts into words what the Ardagh chalice expresses in the shimmering patterns of Celtic art.

Sancti venite,	Approach, you who are holy,
Christi corpus sumite,	Receive the body of Christ,
Sanctum bibentes	Drinking the sacred blood
quo redempti sanguinem.	By which you were redeemed.

Salvati Christi
Corpore et Sanguine,
a quo refecti
laudes dicamus Deo.

Saved by the body
And blood of Christ
Now nourished by it,
Let us sing praises unto God.

Hoc sacramento
Corporis et Sanguinis
omnes exuti
ab inferno faucibus.

By this sacrament
Of the body and blood
All are rescued
From the power of hell.

Dator salutis
Christus, Filius Dei
mundum salvavit
per crucem et sanguinem.

The giver of salvation,
Christ, the Son of God,
Redeemed the world
By his cross and blood.

Pro universis
immolatus Dominus
Ipse sacerdos
existit et hostia.

For the whole world
The Lord is offered up ;
He is at the same time
High priest and victim.

Lege praeceptum
immolari hostias,
qua adumbrantur
divina mysteria.

In the law it is commanded
To immolate victims :
By it were foreshadowed
These sacred mysteries.

Lucis indultor
et Salvator omnium
praeclaram sanctis
largitus est gratiam.

The giver of all light,
And the saviour of all,
Now bestows upon the holy
An exceeding grace.

Accedant omnes
pura mente creduli,
sumant aeternam
salutis custodiam.

Let all approach
In the pure simplicity of faith ;
Let them receive the eternal
Preserver of their souls.

Sanctorum custos,
Rector quoque Dominus,
vitae perennis
largitor credentibus.

The guardian of the saints,
The supreme Ruler & Lord,
The bestower of eternal life,
On those who believe in Him.

Coelestem panem	To the hungry he gives to eat
dat esurientibus,	Of the heavenly food ;
de fonte vivo	To the thirsty he gives to drink
praebet sitientibus.	From the living fountain.

Alpha et Omega,	The Alpha and Omega,
Ipse Christus Dominus	Our Lord Christ Himself
venit, venturus	Now comes : He who shall one day come
iudicare homines.	To judge all mankind.

Now the monastery of Bangor, set beside the sea on the shores of Belfast Lough and founded by St. Comgall in 559, was no isolated desert cut off from the rest of the world. It was one of the great centres from which men went out on heroic and far-reaching missionary journeys. From Bangor, St. Moluag went to Scotland, settling on the island of Lismore in 562, a year before St. Columcille came to Iona, and later, St. Maelrubha who was to make another great foundation at Applecross in Ross-shire in 673. Place-names indicate that both these leaders of missions from Bangor in Ulster travelled widely over Scotland and the Hebrides. Even more important was the great continental missionary effort, headed by St. Columbanus and St. Gall, which began in 590, and which also originated from Bangor. So then, the teaching about the Mass and the Blessed Sacrament that is summed up by the *Sancti venite* and the long series of communion antiphons in the Antiphonary of Bangor, was something that was taken by these intrepid adventurers everywhere that they were able to penetrate. It was something that must have radiated out from the long string of foundations that Columbanus and his monks laid across Europe, a string ending in the famous monasteries of St. Gall and Bobbio. They brought a vivid faith in and a deep devotion to the Mass to a Europe in which such devotion had grown cold or was unknown, and set against the intrigue, vice and strife of the warring states of the time, Irish and Christian ideals of holiness and of the purity of conscience with which one should approach communion. It is perhaps not accidental that the diocese of Liège, which was the first to establish the feast of Corpus Christi, had been one of the important centres of the Irish missionaries.

The Bangor Antiphonary's references to the Mass are confined to the *Sancti venite* and an extensive and interesting collection of communion antiphons ; a feature characteristic of the Celtic rite, and itself an indication of the importance attached to frequent communion. Not till the period of the Stowe Missal, do we possess a complete MS. of the liturgy and ritual of the Mass in Celtic Ireland. The Stowe Missal seems to have originated at Tallaght, a monastery of the Céili Dé reform founded by a certain St. Maelruain (died 792). The Missal was written between 792 and 812. It can be taken that it represents the rite in use over central and southern Ireland at that time, a rite that, whilst it has a general shape corresponding to the present Roman one, shows its own Celtic peculiarities. Celtic liturgy drew on Gallican, Mozarabic and oriental sources and added to them its own native piety and inspiration. So the Celtic Mass is marked by the long series of communion antiphons, and by the very elaborate fraction of the consecrated Host, which took place before the recitation of the Pater noster, for example : yet the modern Irish Catholic, if he was transported back to the Mass said in the tiny beehive vaulted oratories which still stand amongst the Irish fields, would have no difficulty in following the ceremony.

The Mass was, of course, said in Latin, but included in the Stowe Missal is a tract written in Irish, which, basing its explanation on the doctrine of the Mystical Body of Christ, explains how the actions and symbols of the Mass tell the whole story of man's salvation.

The altar, this old Irish tract tells us, is the symbol of persecution and the chalice set on it, the figure of the Church founded upon that persecution. In the Celtic rite, as in other early rites and still in a Dominican Low Mass, the chalice was prepared at the beginning of the Mass. Water was poured in first, symbolising the people who have been "poured" into the Church ; then the wine, symbolising Christ's divinity assuming His Manhood. The "Host, then, super altare, i.e., the turtle dove. This is chanted thereat, to wit, Iesus Christus, Alpha et Omega, hoc est principium et finis. A figure of Christ's Body which has been set in the linen sheet of Mary's womb."

The chalice seems to have been covered with two veils, and their successive removal had a symbolic meaning. Covered by both veils up to the time of the epistle, the law of nature was symbolised, then up to the gospel the veiled revelation of Christ in the Old Testament, next at the gospel a partial unveiling to symbolise the clearer revelation of the prophecies foretelling the coming of Christ, finally at the offertory a complete unveiling and elevation of the chalice to symbolise the full revelation of the New Testament.

The full revelation. The liturgy swept on to the moment of consecration. "Quando canitur : Accepit Iesus panem, the priest bows himself down thrice to repent of his sins. He offers it (the chalice) to

God (and chants Miserere mei Deus), and the people kneel, and here no voice cometh lest it disturb the priest, for this is the right of it, that his mind separate not from God while he chants this lesson. Hence its nomen is periculosa oratio."

The words "periculosa oratio" seem to have been written in the margin of the text of the Canon of the Mass to put the priest on his guard at this moment. Heavy penalties were laid down for those who stumbled over the words of consecration.

After the consecration, the priest took three steps away from the altar and three back to it, for this "is the triad in which everyone sins, in word, in thought, in deed" and so separates oneself from Christ.

The tract goes on to say that the priest examining the chalice and the Host is the figure of the insults and buffets to which Christ was subjected, "the Host on the paten is Christ's Flesh on the tree of the cross," and the fraction of the host, the breaking of that Body with nails on the cross. The meeting of the broken particles of the Host is the figure of the Resurrection, whilst the dipping of a fragment into the chalice is the symbol of Christ's Body immersed in His Blood after His wounding on the cross.

The actual breaking of the Host was an elaborate little ceremony in itself. It seems to have been the custom of the Celtic Church that when a simple priest celebrated Mass, another joined him to assist at the fraction, but a bishop always broke the Host alone. The number of particles into which It was divided varied with the different feasts, each number with its own symbolism, and they were then arranged in a cross pattern, from the different sections of which the different classes of communicants—priests, hermits, children, married people and so on —received communion. The symbolism and its meaning is detailed by the Stowe Missal tract, which ends with the dispositions necessary in those receiving communion. They ought to meditate upon the symbols of the Mass, to realise the "portion of the Host which you receive to be as it were a member of Christ from His cross." Finally, there is the rather Celtic bit of reasoning that it is not right to swallow the Host without tasting it, because one should try to bring savour into God's mysteries, but equally, the Host must not be allowed to go under the back-teeth because one should not dispute too much over these mysteries and run the risk of heresy thereby. The idea is based on the Mystical Body of Christ, that the Church may be torn apart by heresies as a man tears with his teeth.

The Leabhar Breac, the Speckled Book, is a compilation made from older sources at the end of the 14th or the beginning of the 15th century. In it, is another version of this Irish tract on the Mass, which adds to the symbolism of the Stowe Missal tract in saying that the church building which shelters both altar and congregation is the figure "of that human divine shelter, of which is said 'sub umbra alarum tuarum protege me'." It goes on to stress first of all the reality of the offering of the Body and Blood of Christ on the altar and then to refer to the Virgin birth and Mary. "The body which was born of the Virgin Mary, without any stain, without destruction of her virginity, without opening of the womb, without presence of man, and which was crucified by the unbelieving Jews out of spite and envy, and which arose after three days from death, and sits upon the right hand of God the Father in heaven, in glory and in dignity before the angels in heaven. It is the body the same as it is in this great glory, which the righteous consume off God's table, that is, off the holy altar. For this body is the rich viaticum of the faithful, who journey through the paths of pilgrimage and repentance of this world to the heavenly fatherland. This is the seed of the resurrection in the life eternal to the righteous."

In some Irish churches, Mass seems to have been celebrated every day, in others only upon Sundays and feast days. It normally took place early in the morning. The general practice seems to have been frequent communion and this was usually but not always received under both species. The necessity to receive communion in order to keep the soul alive and in health is even stressed by a ruling in the Celtic penitentials, that a penance should not be imposed which would keep the penitent away from communion for too long to his soul's hurt by "fasting from its medicine." The same idea is expressed in another way in the Irish Law tracts, showing the importance of the Mass to the country's welfare. The tracts list certain essentials which could not be done without and which therefore could not be distrained on for debts. They include a milch cow and a plough ox, and the requisites for celebrating Mass.

St. Columbanus laid down that, before going to receive communion, one should make a careful examination of conscience and confession, for the altar is a tribunal and the body of Christ on it will judge those who approach it unworthily. It is not enough, Columbanus wrote, to be free from the capital sins, it is also necessary to "abstain from and wash away the indeterminate vices and fevers of the sick soul before the conjunction of true peace and the covenant of eternal salvation." He ordered his monks to make three prostrations as they approached the altar to receive communion.

Further evidence of Irish reverence for the Mass and the consecrated species comes from the Penitentials to which reference has already been made. The Celtic Church insisted on frequent confession and drew up handbooks listing sins and the appropriate penances to be imposed. Irish missionaries scattered these little books broadcast over Europe and they seem to have a good deal to do with the way in which Catholic indulgences came to develop later on, following out the careful tariffs of sins which were laid down in them and their various possible commutations. The 7th century Penitential of Cummean has an exhaustive section "Of questions concerning the Host," which deals with all possible situations and mishaps. Priests often seem to have carried It about in highly decorated and jewelled chrismals, not merely when taking It to the sick but on their ordinary missionary journeys. Special penances were laid down for anyone who lost the chrismal, and if a person broke into a place where one was kept, it was not only necessary to make sevenfold restitution but to do hard penance on a pilgrimage out of Ireland for five years.

The Stowe Missal includes the order for the visitation of the sick and their reception of communion : so vital was the reception of viaticum before death, that the legends of the Irish saints include miracles in which a saint raises a man to life in order that he may be able to receive communion before he does finally die.

The Blessed Sacrament seems to have been normally kept reserved in the Celtic churches, and it has been suggested that the model of Solomon's temple which was stolen from Clonmacnoise was used as a tabernacle. It had been given to Clonmacnoise by Maelseachlainn, an Irish prince who died in 1020, and its making had cost "a hide from every holding in Meath." The Rule of Ailbe gives one indication of the reverence for the reserved Sacrament which must be shown :—

> "A genuflection thrice, earnestly, after going in past the altar-
> rail, without frivolity and without excitement, going into the
> presence of the king of the angels."

The King of the angels, and the miracle of Christianity is that men, men who still sin against Him, may yet be His friends. Even the saints sin at times—one of John Cassian's desert friends pointed out that otherwise they could hardly truthfully pray "Forgive us our trespasses." This is the appalling intimacy of the Mass, God Himself stooping down to men, circled by legions of angels. There is an instruction on the Sacraments in the Leabhar Breac, which brings this idea clearly, and exhorting people to go to Mass says "Woe indeed to a heart, if great necessity does not hinder him from it, that comes not to the church at the hour of performing this oblation to meet Jesus Christ and the family (muintir) of heaven, to bewail his sins and to (obtain) mercy for them, and to ask help for his soul."

Now the word in the Irish that is used for the family of heaven is *muintir*, the same word that was used to indicate the family of monks around their abbot. It is something intimate, a group bound closely and familiarly together; a Celtic tribute to the reality of the fact that Christians on earth are indeed the fellow citizens of the saints.

If we look for the source of the energy and drive of the Celtic saints, it is to the Mass that we need to turn, and to their vivid faith in it and in the Blessed Sacrament. One of the Antiphonary of Bangor communion antiphons gives the keys to the courage and enterprise of the Irish monks who set out to preach Christ wherever a road or a ship would take them.

"Corpus Domini accepimus, et sanguine ejus potati sumus, ab omni malo non timebimus, quia Dominus nobiscum est.

They had taken the Body of the Lord and drunk His Blood and now they need be afraid of no evil for the Lord was with them.

Set around the Mass, like the carvings that decorate the high crosses or the jewels on the Ardagh chalice, is the Divine Office. The Mass, Christ, is the source of the power of Christian prayer, prayer which ought, like a Celtic lorica, to circle the whole day in a pattern of praise and thanksgiving and intercession and petition.

The Divine Office as we now know it has a long history. Its origins go back to the Old Testament, seven times a day will I praise Thee says the 118th Psalm, which was the special favourite psalm of the Celtic Church, and the 54th Psalm mentions prayer at morning, mid-day and evening. There was a regular series of services through the day in the Jewish synagogues, which the Christians used, at the very beginning, to attend; and they naturally carried over this idea into the new Christian liturgy that was coming into being. The desert monks took the idea further and a regular series of "hours" came into existence, to begin with varying in content from place to place but eventually becoming uniform for the whole Church.

The basis of the Divine Office is scripture, in particular the psalms which make up the bulk of it, and a series of lessons from the Bible together with prayers and hymns. The Celtic saints had a very deep devotion to the psalms and often added the daily recitation of the Three Fifties (the 150 psalms) as a private devotion in addition to the singing of the canonical hours. This Hebrew poetry is for all times and all places ; once you begin to get to know it, it comes back like a melody, fitting in with unexpected scenes and places, David's verse insinuating itself into an Irish landscape as though it had been written specially for this land that he had never seen. St. Augustine pointed out how the meaning of the psalms would come home to anyone who began to try and live up to their teaching, and this poetry will not stale with repetition, rather sudden new meanings and vistas open out on each recitation.

The Celtic Church loved to penetrate the meaning of the psalms, not content with the surface, the literal and historical sense, but reaching out after the spiritual senses, applying to Christ and to the life of every Christian. The Celtic Church knew and used most of the Latin commentaries of the Fathers on the psalms. A fragment of an Old Irish commentary, dating from around 850, has survived, it details the different senses in which scripture is to be understood : it gives a rather attractive description of the Book of Psalms to begin with :—

"This book is one and is manifold, to wit, the form of one book without, and many psalms within, like some city which one wall surrounds without and many buildings within. In such wise is the Psalter, to wit, the form of one book without and many psalms within, like some glorious building with many shrines, with various treasure houses with special keys to open each one of them. There is however a special key before each psalm, to wit, its title."

Then too in the mysterious economy of God, these psalms were written by divine inspiration, and the man who sings and prays them is praising God with poetry that came direct from Him.

There is no evidence to indicate that the same number of "Hours" were celebrated uniformly all over Ireland. An Irish note in a Trinity College MS. gives the primitive Eastern office and does not mention Prime, which is included in the Antiphonary of Bangor. Compline seems to date, at the earliest, from the 9th century. There were Irish names for the canonical hours :—Prime was *antert* (ante tertiam), before Terce, which was *Tert*, then came *Sest* (Sext) and None, called *médon lai* (mid-day). From the Latin Verspertina came the Irish *fescer* or *espartain*, at midnight was *midnoct* or *iarmérge*, and at dawn *maten* or *gairm an choilig* (cockcrow). The longest was this last, dawn office and its length varied with that of the night. St. Columbanus gives details of the way in which he, for his monks in Europe, and presumably Bangor in Ireland from which he came, arranged this office. For Saturday and Sunday, from November 1 to March 25, he had 75 psalms and 25 antiphons, one antiphon to a set of three psalms. Then, from March 25 to June 24, as the nights shortened, a group of three psalms and an antiphon were dropped each week, so reducing the number eventually to 36 psalms and 12 antiphons. The process was reversed as the nights grew longer again. For the rest of the week, Columbanus had 24 psalms in summer and 36 in winter, but there is no evidence to indicate whether or not he had a sliding scale between this maximum and minimum too.

Just as the Church's liturgy with its cycle of feasts recapitulates and relives the life of Christ through the year, so a mystical meaning was attached to the times of the canonical hours. The Irish MS. mentioned above explains :—

"Why is celebration made at these hours rather than at other hours ? Not hard to say. Terce, because it was then Christ was given up by Pontius Pilate, and therein grace came upon the Apostles. Sext, for then Adam sinned and then Christ was placed upon the cross, None, for then He yielded up His spirit. Vespers and Sext, the same course of evil therein, for offering used to made in them according to the law. Nocturns, however, for then the elements were created. Matins, for then Peter denied, and used to shed tears of blood then always, and then Christ was beaten in the house of Caiaphas."

If the symbolism seems a little far-fetched, the prayers for the canonical hours in the Antiphonary of Bangor put the matter in a different light, and set the symbols in proper perspective and make them a matter of moment and urgency for ourselves. The Holy Spirit came down on the Apostles at the third hour ; we can ask for its grace too :—

"Tibi subnexis precibus Christo Domino supplicamus, qui in hora tertia Diei Spiritum Sanctum Apostolis orantibus emisisti, ejusdem gratiae participationem nobis poscentibus jubeas concedi. Qui regnas."

The Antiphonary of Bangor, in addition to these prayers in prose, has a series of rhymed couplets for the different hours. At Sext, the crucifixion is recalled :—

"Tuis parce supplicibus
Sexta hora orantibus
Qui fuisti pro omnibus
Christi in cruce positus."

None was also the hour at which the centurion Cornelius had been visited by the angel. Just as Cornelius' prayers had been heard, so too we can beg audience for ours :—

> "Exaudi preces omnium
> Nona hora orantium
> In qua Christe Cornelium
> Visitasti per angelum."

At midnight, we cry out again to Christ, recalling His omnipotent power which loosed Peter from his chains :—

> "Jesu clementer visita
> Nocte orantes media
> Qua divina potentia
> Petri solvisiti vincula."

At Matins, as the eastern sky begins to lighten, we can ask for the coming of the Sun of Righteousness, for the light of Christ, to come to us :—

> "Deus Qui pulsis tenebris
> Diei lucem tribuis,
> Adventum veri luminis
> Tuis effunde famulis."

Another prayer for Matins, this time in prose, uses staccato invocations to Christ, hope and health, life and spirit, help in tribulation, defender of our souls :—

> "Tu es spes et salus. Tu es vita et virtus. Tu es adjutor in tribulationibus. Tu es defensor animarum nostrarum, Deus Israel in omnibus. Qui regnas."

For Prime, the Antiphonary includes a beautiful collect which dedicates the whole day to God, asking Him to be our protector throughout the whole day, helper, leader, light of our hearts. It asks Him to take care of our thoughts and words and deeds, so that we shall be able to please him and carry out His will and walk in the straight road for all our lifetime.

> "Esto nobis protector in ista die ; Domine sancte, Pater omni-potens, Aeterne Deus et miserator et misericors, et auxiliator, et dux nobis et inluminator cordium nostrorum. Custodi Domine cogitationes, sermones, opera, ut possimus placere in conspectu tuo Domine, et perficere voluntatem tuam, et ambulare in via recta toto nostrae vitae tempore."

The collects for Vespers include this short but very beautiful prayer, in which is suggested a kind of exchange between earth and heaven, our prayers rising up to God and His blessing coming down upon us. "Vespertina oratio nostra ascendat ad aures divinae majestatis tuae, et descendat benedictio tua Domine super nos, quemadmodum speravimus in te. Qui regnas."

The Antiphonary of Bangor includes a collection of hymns which were also included in the Divine Office. The "Gloria in Excelsis" was to be sung at vespers and at matins, this last is its original place, for it was to begin with a dawn hymn and only later was inserted into the liturgy of the Mass. The "Te Deum" was sung on Sundays at Bangor. But there were also metrical hymns and the Irish seem to have quickly taken to their composition. Hymn writing in the West is supposed to have been begun by St. Hiliary of Poitiers (died 366). He had been in exile in the East and had there realised their propaganda value, the heretic Arius had composed songs that ordinary men could sing—and propagate his heresy thereby. But St. Ambrose of Milan (died 397) was the first to write really popular hymns, Hilary's seem to have been a little too theological in content. Ambrose too is said to have introduced antiphonal singing by two choirs to the West, it also had come from the East and is thought to have originated at Antioch.

Considering Irish devotion to St. Martin and the latter's connection with St. Hilary, it is not surprising to find one of the Antiphonary of Bangor's hymns attributed to the latter. Whether there is any truth in the attribution is another matter, the hymn is a simple little piece telling the story of the life of Christ. The Rule of Ailbe says that it used to be sung when the bell was rung for the canonical hours, and indeed to recall the principal facts of the Incarnation is as good a way as any to prepare for prayer.

The Bangor hymns for Holy Communion and in honour of the martyrs have already been mentioned, another seems to be intended for the blessing of the Paschal candle, if it was not used daily when the lamps were lit in the evening. One of the most attractive is that for the midnight office. It brings out very clearly the vivid sense of symbolism that the Celtic monks had and how they realised that the events of the Old Testament foreshadowed those of the New. The setting is easy to imagine, the surf growling to itself on the strand at Bangor, or perhaps the still glitter of moonlight upon the Shannon at Clonmacnoise, or the wind screaming over the stone built beehive roofs of one of the island hermitages. It is dark and the night is mysterious and silent. So the hymn recalls the striking down of the first born of Egypt, all but the Jews who were protected by the blood of the paschal lamb. We too, Christians, are protected by the Blood of Christ, the real Paschal Lamb that the Passover one prefigured, from all danger. In the dark we keep vigil, like the wise virgins, and then recalling Paul and Silas in prison, the metaphor changes to that of the prison of this world in which we lie bound by sin and cry out for the help of God.

The Divine Office of the Celtic Church was not just a matter of singing and praying. The whole man took part in the work and there were numerous genuflections and prostrations. The Rule of Ailbe gives an indication of these :—

"A hundred genuflections for him at the Beati (the 118th Psalm) at the beginning of the day before his questions, thrice fifty (psalms) dearer than (other) works, with a hundred genuflections every hour of vespers.

"A hundred genuflections every matin are due in the church of a believer from the feast of John whom they adore unto the solemn pasch of abstinence."

From the "Rule of the Grey Monks" comes the picture of the Celtic monks making his way out to the church on a dark night when the wind has a nip in it and the sea is breaking angrily along the coast.

"To go to *iamérge*, great labour ; the wind stings my two ears ; were it not dread of the blessed Lord, though sweet the bell, I would not go to it."

"Fear of the blessed Lord." It is easy to think of the Divine Office, of any church service, as something a little unreal, out of touch with the main work of the world outside. Yet, in fact, it is the opposite, the psalms and hymns and prayers are an approach to ultimate reality, to the source of all being, to Truth itself. These praises are a foretaste of the shout of joy of heaven, these prayers the essential link in our getting what we need to live here and now. For the Celtic saints, the Mass and the Divine Office were the great actions of the day, the source of power on which everything else depended and from which every other activity took its origin and direction.

Chapter Seven

THE SON OF THE VIRGIN

SET on the short green turf of Iona of St. Columcille, beside the ancient abbey church and between the clear sea shading from the white sands into depths of jade and sapphire, and the grey rocks which rise sharply in the little hills of the islands, is the high cross of St. Martin. It dates from the 10th century, yet still the bosses and plaits and intertwining beasts of its Celtic artist's imagination stand out boldly and clearly in the bright Hebridean sunshine. One side is entirely covered with such designs, the other, more worn, includes some panels showing scenes from scripture, the lions' den with Daniel and David playing before Saul. Above them, in the place of honour at the intersection of the arms of the cross, Our Lady is shown, enthroned and holding her Child, circled by adoring angels.

Southward from Iona lies the island of Islay, and here again is another carving of the same scene upon a magnificent high cross. The Kildalton cross of Islay includes among its other panels, one showing the sacrifice of Isaac: the Old Testament prefiguring of the sacrifice of the cross, the Passion of Mary's Son. The lichened carvings of the Hebrides bring us back almost with a jerk to a realisation of the devotion of the Celtic Church to the Virgin, the "virginal, strong diadem, the holy mother of my Prince" as Oengus the Culdee described her in his Martyrology (c. 800).

Devotion to Our Lady is, naturally, something that has grown steadily with the passing of time. That was only to be expected—at the very beginning the shattering fact of the Resurrection overshadowed everything else, even the Woman who had stood at the foot of the cross and alone had then understood what was really happening. It was to her Son that the early Church had first to turn, to define its teaching about Him exactly against the early heresies which denied either His

69

Divinity or His Humanity. These definitions about the Son led naturally to His mother : in 431, the Council of Ephesus formally declared as an article of the Catholic Faith that Mary was truly the mother of God. The next year, Patrick landed at Saul in Ireland to begin his mission, and, while we have no definite information on the subject, it seems likely that the new definition would be an important part of his preaching. Tradition says that he picked shamrock leaves to teach the doctrine of the Trinity to his hearers and tradition is very likely right, for Patrick stresses belief in the Trinity in his "Confession." The Arian heresy, which denied the divinity of Christ, was still very much alive, and St. Patrick needed to make quite clear to the Irish both that Christ was God and that Mary was His mother.

Whatever may have been the details of St. Patrick's sermons, the Celtic Church took a firm hold on these two articles of Catholic doctrine, so that you find them woven through its prayers and hymns, so intimately that the words may slip past before you realise all their implications. The Antiphonary of Bangor's prayers were mostly addressed to the Second Person of the Trinity, as indicated by the "Qui regnas" of the doxology at the end of each of them, and this had been a custom observed elsewhere in the Church against the Arians. Then, turning to Christ's humanity and the reality of the Incarnation, Irish hymns and litanies and prayers repeat over and over again the same title that the cross of St. Martin illustrates, "Son of the Virgin, Mary's great Son." The hymn traditionally ascribed to St. Fiacc but whose real date appears to be c. 800, speaks of St. Patrick's joy in being "in the service of Mary's Son." The Bangor hymns include one for Sunday Matins, and almost certainly of Irish composition, which in short sparkling verses which carry an echo of the Nicene Creed, gathers up these ideas, stressing the Trinity, Christ "light from light" and then inevitably going on to sing of the Incarnation and the Virgin birth and Mary.

The Trinity, Christ, God and Man, Mary His Mother, these were the accents of belief of the Celtic Church, touchstones of orthodoxy, the very opposite of the Protestant attempt to snatch the Child from the arms of His mother. The whole concept blazes forth in the shattering picture of Our Lady in the Book of Kells, "the chief relic of the Western World" as the Annalists called it. The Book of Kells dates from the 8th century ; it was perhaps begun in Iona (which was later to put the same picture on its high cross) and completed in Ireland, to which it may have been taken to escape the Viking raids. It has a whole page drawing of Our Lady, seated on a throne and holding her Child : the Enthroned Madonna that appeared after Ephesus, the artists' attempt to symbolise the Mother of God. To us, reared on the saccharine sweetness of modern statues of Our Lady, the Kells picture will come as a shock, its Byzantine stiffness, the regal woman dressed in purple with the strange, almost masculine face, and elaborately braided golden hair. Her Child, dressed in green, has the face of a grown man, one hand raised as if in blessing, the other, an attractive touch, resting gently on His mother's. Four angels occupy the corners of the design, the whole being enclosed in an elaborate border of Celtic ornament ; opposite, the text, almost unreadable in the splendour of its decoration, tells how Christ was born in Bethlehem and the Magi came to offer gifts.

If you look again at the Kells picture, you will begin to like it and see in the formal majesty of Mary the bright courage that gave her consent to become the mother of Christ and take the hard road that led both Him and her to Calvary.

Oengus the Culdee put something of this concept into the words with which he commemorated Christmas in his Martyrology :—"At great marvellous Christmas, Christ from white pure Mary was born, with the ruin of darkness, (Christ) the luminous king of Adam's race." In another place he compared Pilate's wife with Mary and brought in the circling angels of Iona and Kildalton and the Book of Kells. Pilate's wife, haughty in life, was now forgotten, mouldering in the grave. "Not so is Mary the Virgin, beloved is her strong fortress : Adam's race, a lofty ambit, magnifies her, with a host of angels."

Perhaps one should take a hint from the dedication of the Iona cross to Martin and go back to that saint's devotion to Our Lady in any consideration of the Celtic Church's devotion to her. Celtic Ireland knew well Sulpicius Severus' account of how he and another monk had heard voices from Martin's cell, in which Martin was apparently alone. When Martin came out, Sulpicius with great difficulty eventually got him to admit that Mary and Sts. Thecla and Agnes had been with him, furthermore that they were his frequent visitors. If the Irish people now flock to the village of Knock, where Mary is alleged to have appeared, the Celtic Church on its first coming to Ireland must have been equally familiar with the idea of her occasional appearances.

The Culdees, or Céili Dé, of which Oengus quoted above was one, seem to have had a very special and particular devotion to Mary. An ancient MS. written between 831 and 840 gives an account of the customs of St. Maelruain's monastery of Céili Dé at Tallaght, and of the sayings of that saint and his disciple, Maeldithruib. The Céili Dé were asked why they were so continually singing the Magnificat. The answer, with a real Irish twist to it, was that it was fitting that the song which had come from the head of the Virgin Mary when she had conceived by the Holy Ghost, should be set as a crown on the chant in praise of God. Another Tallaght MS. says that just as work done for a king should be gilt and decorated, so we should gild our work for God with the Magnificat.

There is a long and rather confusingly detailed account of Maeldithruib's method of prayer. The Céili Dé, like all the Irish saints, had a great love of the Three Fifties (the psalms) and their daily recitation. Maeldithruib, and perhaps with him all the Céili Dé of Tallaght, inserted "Sancte Michael, ora pro nobis ; Sancta Maria, ora pro nobis" between every two psalms of the 150, adding an invocation to the saint whose feast day it might happen to be. He sang a special hymn to St. Michael in the evening and to Mary in the morning, to invoke their protection.

St. Moling (died 697), founder of St. Mullins on the River Barrow in Ireland, was one of the favourite patron saints of the later Céili Dé. The story goes that he once escaped from his enemies by singing an Irish litany of the saints, beginning with St. Brigit and ending with Our Lady. One Irish litany, or rather invocation by a long series of titles, of Our Lady has survived : in its present form it is thought to be 12th century. It begins "O Great Mary, O Mary, greatest of Marys" and continues at length calling her, for instance, Mistress of the Heavens, Mother of Eternal Glory, Mother of the Heavenly and Earthly Church, Beauty of Virgins, Star of the Sea, Cancelling of Eve's disgrace, Beauty of Women, Chief of Virgins, Temple of the Living God, Sanctuary of the Holy Spirit, Cedar of Mount Lebanon, Cypress of Mount Sion, Crimson Rose of the Land of Jacob and Noblest Born of the Christian Flock. This old invocation, which is included in the Leabhar Breac, lays very great stress on Mary's purity, perpetual virginity and fullness of grace ; rather similar titles are given her in an Irish hymn to Our Lady, beginning "A Muire min maithingen"—"O Gentle Mary, good daughter." This hymn is traditionally ascribed to St. Columcille though actually of very much later date.

The Celtic Martyrologies mark a number of feasts of Our Lady, including Candlemas, the Visitation, the Assumption and her Nativity. It was thought until recently that the Celtic Church had been the first to keep the feast of Mary's Conception, but this belief has now been shown to be quite without foundation. The Bobbio Missal, a continental missal of the 7th or 8th century and composed from mingled Irish and Gallican sources, gives two special Masses of Our Lady, January 18, In sanctae Maria Solemnitate ; and for the feast of the Assumption, In adsumptione sanctae Maria. The Preface for the latter Mass brings out the contrast between Eve and Mary—the new Eve. A faint sidelight on early devotion to Mary in Ireland may be gained by the link with Alcuin (died 804), who is thought to have been a student of Clonmacnoise on the Shannon. The dedication of Saturday to Our Lady is an ancient custom and the little collection of Masses left by Alcuin includes two votive ones of the Virgin Mary for Saturday. Perhaps Ireland already observed this custom then.

Mary, very naturally, appears again and again in Celtic art, both on the high crosses and on some of the Celtic reliquaries—including the Domhnach Airgid, the Miosach and that for Columcille's Cathach or psalter on which she is shown with St. John standing by the Cross. The Book of Kells picture seems to be the earliest of the series. Incidents from the Gospel story appear on the high crosses in Ireland : at Moone she is to be seen riding on an ass, holding her Child and with St. Joseph walking alongside—the Flight into Egypt. Duleek has a group of the Holy Family and the Annunciation and Visitation. Muiredach's cross at Monasterboice shows the Adoration of the Magi—Mary is seated with her Child, the star shining above her head, the Three Magi approach together with a fourth figure who is probably their angel guide of Byzantine tradition. In Scotland, the great cross of Ruthwell shows the Annunciation, Visitation, and the Flight into Egypt. At Brechin, a famous church site of the Celtic Church, there is a cross slab bearing a Latin cross at whose intersection is a medallion of Our Lady with the Child. The identification is clinched here, as at Ruthwell, by an inscription, in Hiberno-Saxon minuscules :—$\bar{s}$ maria $\overline{mr}$ $\chi \bar{pi}$ (S. Mary, Mother of Christ). Above Our Lady is shown a dove, presumably symbolising the Holy Spirit, below are two figures, one of which has been thought to be St. Peter. The background of the cross contains the symbols of the Four Evangelists. This Brechin slab would therefore seem to sum up, in a symbolic design, the Virgin Birth, Mary's motherhood of God and her close link with the Church with Peter at its head, and with the Gospel history.

Most of the Rosary mysteries are to be found on the high crosses, and must then, as now, have been subjects of prayer and meditation, for these carvings were meant for popular instruction. Moreover, the Celtic Church looked into the deeper symbolism and meaning of these scenes. For example, a homily in the Leabhar Breac explains the symbolic meaning of the picture of the Adoration of the Magi, which one may see at Monasterboice. The Magi represent all nations coming to find Christ, guided by the star which is the light of the gospel, and finding the Child in His mother's arms, Mary standing here as a type of the Church. The Rule of Ailbe links up with this, with its outspoken reference to the Church as our mother :—

"Their Father is noble God, their Mother is Holy Church : let it not be mouth-humility ; let each have compassion on his brother."

To gather up into one statement the teaching of the Celtic Church about Mary and its devotion to her, it is only necessary to turn to the splendid hymn of Cú-chuimne. Cú-chuimne seems to have been a monk of Iona and to have died in 747. His hymn has been described as the finest surviving example of Irish-Latin versification. In it, the glitter of Latin verse is wedded to the Irish sparkle of assonance and internal rhyme, to tell of Mary's fame and privileges, of the Annunciation and of her perpetual virginity, the contrast between her obedience and Eve's disobedience, and finally to beg her help to bring us safely to heaven. The text of the hymn reads :—

Cantemus in omni die concinentes varie,
Conclamantes Deo dignum hymnum sanctae Mariae.

Bis per chorum hinc et inde collaudamus Mariam,
Ut vox pulset omnem aurem per laudem vicariam.

Maria de tribu Juda, summi mater Domini,
Opportunam dedit curam aegrotanti homini.

Gabriel advexit verbum sinu Patris paterno,
Quod conceptum et susceptum in utero materno.

Haec est summa, haec est sancta, virgo venerabilis,
Quae ex fide non recessit sed extitit stabilis.

Huic matri nec inventa ante nec post similis
Nec de prole fuit plane humanae originis.

Per mulierem et lignum mundus prius periit,
Per mulieris virtutem, ad salutem rediit.

Maria mater miranda patrem suum edidit,
Per quem aqua late lotus totus mundus credidit.

Haec concepit margaritam, non sunt vana somnia,
Pro qua sane Christiani vendunt sua omnia.

Tunicam per totum textam Christo mater fecerat,
Quae peracta Christi morte, sorte statim steterat.

Induamus arma lucis loricam et galeam,
Ut simus Deo perfecti, suscepti per Mariam.

Amen, Amen, adjuramus merita puerperae,
Ut non possit flamma pyrae nos dirae decerpere.

Christi nomen invocemus angelis sub testibus,
Ut fruamur et scribamur litteris colestibus.

Cantemus in omni die etc.*

From devotion to Mary, it is natural to turn to Irish devotion to the saints, whose queen she is. Sometimes the Irish litanies invoke her as the special leader of women saints and virgins, as in the famous Broom of Devotion of Colga Ua Duinechda (died 796) whose petitions, addressed to Christ, include "I beseech with thee all the female saints, virgins, of the whole world around Mary, Virgin, around thy holy mother herself." In the entry for All Saints' Day in the Martyrology of Gorman (composed between 1166 and 1174), the whole host of heaven stands grouped around Mary :—

"On the venerable day of Allhallowtide behold ye the Lord Himself, the angels, a mystical band, and all the saints of heaven, hosts with clear white purity, around great honourable Mary."

Irish devotion to the saints in heaven was extraordinarily vivid, as indeed it still is in the more remote country districts especially. It is still easy to meet people who speak as familiarly of the Celtic saints as of the local postman. The Cross has indeed won victory over death, the saint in heaven is still very close to his friends here on earth and able to be of much more help to them than he was before he died. So

*A metrical translation exists of this hymn, following the meaning fairly closely whilst attempting to model itself on the original metre and rhyme structure. It is given in the Appendix at the end of this Book.

not only the lorica prayers but long litanies of the saints are characteristic of Irish private prayers of the period of the Celtic Church. They invoke not only the great names of the universal Church in general and of the Celtic Church in particular, but also all the numberless saints whose names and identity are known only to God :—the monks around famous Irish monastic founders, companies of pilgrims and the like. There is a suggestion that real sanctity is the normal outcome of the monastic life in petitions like :—

I invoke :—

"Seven hundred true monks who were hidden in Rathan before Mochuta went on his course of exile to Lesmór.   Per Iesum."

"Eight hundred men who occupied Lesmór with Mochuta, each third one of them a man of the grace of God.   Per Iesum."

Or the rather amusing :—

"The monks of Fintan Mac Úi Echach : they fed on nothing but herbs of the earth and water.

"There is not room to enumerate them because of their multitude. Eight Fintans among them.   Per Iesum."

Or again :—

"Four thousand monks with the grace of God under the yoke of Comgall of Benchor (Bangor).   Per Iesum."

The same litany asks the help of foreigners who had come on pilgrimage to Ireland, some temporarily, some to settle. The fame of the Irish monasteries and their schools brought crowds of students and pilgrims, and quite a number seem to have taken up permanent residence in the country. So this particular litany begins with the invocation of one such group :—

"Thrice fifty coracles of Roman pilgrims who landed in Erin with Ele, with Notal, with Neman the venerable, with Corconutain.   Per Iesum."

Tied up with this very vivid sense of the unity of the Church in heaven with that on earth, is an equally vivid belief in the need for prayers for those of the dead who were not so saintly and might be spending some time in purgatory. The 9th century "Rule of the Céili Dé" says that "There is nothing that a man does on behalf of the soul of one who dies that does not help it, whether vigil or abstinence, or requiem or frequent benediction."

Devotion to the saints led beyond the lists of the litanies to special hymns to particular saints, in honour of Patrick, Columcille, Brigit and so on. Ultan's hymn in honour of St. Brigit of Kildare may go back to the 7th century. It is in Irish with the last verse in Latin and includes these stanzas :—

"Brigit, ever excellent woman, golden sparkling flame,
lead us to the eternal Kingdom, the dazzling resplendent sun.

May Brigit deliver us past throngs of devils :
may she break before us the battles of every plague!

The true virgin, dear, with vast dignity,
I shall be safe always with my saint of Leinster."

There was, too, devotion to the angels, and hymns and prayers composed in their honour. Today, we seldom think about the reality of the existence of the angels, and it comes almost as a surprise in wandering over the territory of the Celtic Church to come on the numerous ancient dedications to St. Michael. Michael is the patron of high places, of the Skellig Rock off the coast of Kerry in Ireland, and of Michael's Mount in Cornwall, and of many old church sites set upon headlands, where the wind keens in over them off the sea. St. Michael is the object of a very fine Latin hymn by St. Colman mac Mur-chon. This particular St. Colman seems to have been the abbot of the monastery of Moville on the shores of Strangford Lough who died in 736. The hymn seems to have been taken over to Europe and become known there. It begins with a contrast between the omens of paganism and faith in the Trinity, asking St. Michael's help :—

"In Trinitate spes mea fixa non in omine
et archangelum deprecor Michaelem nomine."

The hymn asks the protection of Michael against the devil, especially at the hour of death, and that he will intercede for Colman with God. Then Michael, Gabriel, Raphael, all the angels and archangels and the saints are invoked, both always and at the hour of death, to pray that he may come to the eternal halls of the king of the kingdom and the joys of paradise.

"Sanctus Michael me defendat semper suis viribus
anima egrediente cum sanctorum milibus.

Sanctus Gabriel, sanctus Raphiel atque omnes angeli
intercedant pro me semper simul et archangeli.

Eterna possint prestare regis regni aulia
ut possedeam cum Christo paradisi gaudia."

The Celtic saint then was conscious of never being alone. Saints and
angels went with him about his daily work, whether alone or in a crowd,
whether in the monastic "cities" of Clonmacnoise and Glendalough, or
on some solitary hermitage in a dense wood on the hillside or on an
islet in sea or lake. God, Christ, Mary, and what the Leabhar Breac
calls the "family of heaven" were closer to him than the touch of the
breeze at dawn, or the sting of the breaking sprays over his curragh's
prow.

Chapter Eight

THE SHAPE OF HISTORY

TO follow the tracks of the Celtic saints over Scotland and Ireland is to travel the whole gamut of the countryside, from fertile meadowland to rocky hilltop, from island, where the old chapel lies half-buried in blown sand, to the hermitage still hidden in the wood below the cliff down which a rill of water cascades. But at each site, if there is anything at all left for the stranger to examine, the most likely thing to strike him will be the cross. It may be a cross that is hard to find, cut on the living rock beside a spring, as it is on the edge of the sands in North Uist in the Outer Hebrides, it may be a cross enlivened with a simple but vigorous pattern as upon the many early cross slabs and pillar stones of Ireland, or again, it may be the full flowering of those earlier carvings, the free standing high cross of the 9th and 10th centuries. The range is from the North Uist blessed well where you must run your hand over the rock to find the carving to the splendour of St. Martin's Cross in Iona and Muiredach's in Monasterboice.

The stone is often weathered and the designs hard to make out, until a shower passes and the sun gleams on the wet rock, so that the stiff figures and the elaborate meshes of Celtic ornament stand out as clearly as the day they were first cut. If then, we pick out the meaning of the pictures in the rain-washed sunshine, we shall discover them to present a particular view of human history, not in the light of the sun in the sky but in that of the Sun of Justice, Christ our Lord. The high crosses uphold the view that the shape of history is conditioned by the Cross and that the pattern of events is a meaningful one and not a mere series held together by chance and tending nowhere.

Celtic art had, to begin with, dealt almost entirely in abstract patterns, spirals and knotwork and twisting interlaces. But Christianity is not an abstract religion, it is not a theory that has been fashioned by philosophy, but it is based upon happenings, real happenings, in the real world. Celtic art had, as it became more and more Christian, to take notice of that fact and adapt itself to it, and begin the representation of the events narrated in the Scriptures. The free standing cross is therefore carved all over not only with formal designs, which fill all the remaining space, but with a series of panels each not only telling its own particular story, but each linked with the next in a connected train of thought. The figures tend to be stiff and formalised : the Irish artists seem to have often copied similarly formal designs that they knew from the oriental textiles that came into Ireland at this time, both for use as hangings and wrapped round relics. In fact, the whole subject of carving or painting scenes from scripture had its own conventions, which were laid down for artists to follow, so enabling everybody to read the language of pictures easily and readily.

The crosses were set about the Celtic monasteries, forming their chief ornament. Others were termon crosses, set to mark the boundaries of the monastic lands, or where a fugitive might enter sanctuary. Pilgrims coming to the place would visit the crosses, as they still do on the surviving Irish pilgrimages to these old church sites, and, in all probability, be addressed on the subjects shown in the carved panels. Many of the finest high crosses must have been erected during the period of the Viking attacks on Ireland and Scotland, both a dramatic act of faith and a reminder to the harassed people that God, Who had helped His own in the past, would not forsake them now.

It is the help of God illustrated from the Old Testament, together with the events of the Gospel, that make up the series of pictures on the high crosses. These historical events are linked up with the three vital dates of the Christian view of history :—the Fall of Adam, the Crucifixion and Resurrection, and the Last Judgment. So the usual design that the high cross artists followed was to show the Fall at the base of the cross shaft, then scenes from the Old and New Testaments, and finally on the head of the cross on one side the Crucifixion and on the other the Last Judgment.

It is not a view of history that appeals to us today. The colours are too harsh and the teaching is too harsh, the angel with the sword of fire turning Adam and Eve out of Eden, blood and death and the devil defeated on Calvary, the damned cast into an eternity of pain. Yet in its very violence it gives a pattern and a meaning to history, and to each individual's life. The individual is no longer the victim of chance and fate ; Christianity is a religion of free choice, Adam chose to disobey

God, and so do we ; it is by our own selection and desire that we will go to hell. If, today, we think of hell-fire as an outworn sanction, it is because we do not understand this matter of our free-will and power to choose, the fact that every action of ours here and now echoes into eternity and ennobles the most obscure or wretched life. Nothing that we do or think or say is pointless in the Christian view ; it is every time a choice, for God or against Him, for heaven or for hell.

Man is free to make his own choices, but God remains in complete control of the whole universe, and the source of the power for human decisions comes from Him alone. That God created the world out of nothing, that He maintains it in being and that all events are under the control of His Providence is equally the teaching of the high cross pictures. No matter how hopeless or evil the situation may appear, God is in complete command of it and can save here and now just as he saved Daniel in the lion's den and the children in the fiery furnace in the past.

The selection of incidents to illustrate this theme of the help of God, which is shown on the high crosses, seems to have come in the first place from a Jewish prayer for fast days, which reminded God of how He had saved Noah, Daniel, Jonah and so on in the past, and then asked His help for His people at the present time. St. Cyprian of Antioch, at the end of the 2nd century, adapted this old form of prayer for Christian use, adding a second section which entreated Christ by His miracles—the miracle of the loaves and fishes, the raising of Lazarus, and so on. The whole series naturally had an immediate appeal to the Christian martyrs suffering for their faith and putting their trust in this same help and power of God against all manner of attack.

The Church has retained this ancient form of appeal to God, by inserting it in the form of a litany in the prayers for a departing soul in the Roman Breviary. Ireland put it on her high crosses and mingled it with her prayers. Colga Ua Duinechda's "Broom of Devotion" has already been mentioned, it invokes a number of Old Testament individuals and asks their help, whilst Colman's hymn uses the appeal to the particular events which befell these people in the past :—

"The Prince who protected the three boys out of the fiery furnace
    with redness,
    may He protect us, as He protected David de manu Gólai."

The full development of the high cross and its pictures seems to have originated in the south of Ireland and to have been connected with the

Céili Dé, and it is therefore interesting to find that Oengus the Culdee brings this form of supplication, by recalling historical events, to its highest pitch of expression. At the end of his Martyrology, he prays to the saints he has commemorated, the "kingfolk around the King above the clouds." The appeal takes the form of a litany, first to the saints :—

"O holy troop of the seven heavens, since great is your tenderness, heal my heart for the sake of Mary's Son."

From the saints he turns to Mary's Son Himself and turns the rather bald petitions of the Roman Breviary's *Ordo Commendationis Animae* into a leaping flame of love, mounting to heaven.

"Harken Thou, O Jesus, O Christ, whose servant I am, mayst Thou grant all the prayer of every son of piety!

"The prayer of every son of piety, O Lord, it is not idle : mayst Thou grant (it) to them, if what they pray be fitting.

"If what they pray be fitting, O King that rulest the earth, mayst Thou save their bodies, mayst Thou sanctify their souls!

"The soul of every son of life through Thee has been sanctified ; Adam's race that is highest by Jesus has been saved."

The Breviary prayer merely asks God to save the departing soul as He saved Daniel from the lion's den, and so on. It is instructive to watch Oengus handling the same petitions with a flash of Celtic genius. I set a selection of his Irish verses against the Latin of the Breviary.

Libera Domine animam servi tui, sicut liberasti Noe de deluvio.

Mayst Thou save me, O Jesus, from every ill on earth, as Thou savedst Noah, son of Lamech, from the Flood.

Libera Domine animam servi tui, sicut liberasti Abraham de Ur Chaldaeorum.

Mayst Thou save me, O Jesus, O king of pure brightness, as Thou savedst Abraham from the hands of the Chaldeans.

Libera Domine animam servi tui, sicut liberasti Isaac de hostia, et de manu patris sui Abrahae.

Mayst Thou save me, O Jesus, into Thy many-graced heaven, as Thou savedst Isaac from his father's hands.

Libera Domine animam servi tui, sicut liberasti Petrum et Paulum de carceribus.

Mayst Thou save me, O Jesus, for the sake of Thy martyrs, (as Thou savedst) Peter and Paul before kings, from the punishment of the prison.

These then are the subjects that we shall find upon the high crosses, mingled, on the later examples, with groupings from other sources, particularly from Carolingian ivory carvings which the Irish knew, and which were often arranged to form special groups relating to the feasts, especially to Christmas and Easter. Perhaps the best example to make a start with is the high cross of Muiredach at Monasterboice, which has been claimed as the finest surviving Irish figured cross and on which a definite date, unlike most of the others, can be put.

Monasterboice is a pleasant spot, set in fertile lowland, a little to the north of the River Boyne, and close to many historic sites. Quite near is the ruin of the abbey of Mellifont, the first Cistercian foundation in Ireland : it came to replace the neighbouring Celtic monastery. On the River Boyne itself are the Megalithic tombs of Newgrange, and Slane Hill where Patrick lit his Easter fire, and Tara, are within an easy journey. Two ruined chapels mark the site of Monasterboice, a nearly complete round tower, from whose top one may survey the checkerboard of the Irish fields, and two great high crosses, Muiredach's very well preserved, but the second, taller, example, much weathered.

The name Muiredach is inscribed on the high cross, and this Muiredach has been identified as Muiredach son of Domnall, who was abbot here and also "high steward" of the southern Ui Neill and "chief counsellor" of the people of Bregia. He died in 922, which fixes the date of the high cross that commemorates him. The cross is a solid and rather squat affair, set, as usual, upon a carved base and the whole completely decorated, front, back and sides, both with pictures and with panels of Celtic ornament.

One side is concerned with the Easter mysteries and leads up to the Crucifixion on the head of the cross. The bottom panel shows the arrest of Christ in the garden of Gethsemane. It is interesting to notice that Our Lord wears a cloak secured with a Celtic brooch. The next panel takes us with a sudden bound beyond the events of the first Good Friday and the first Easter morning, to St. Thomas and his doubts about the Resurrection. It shows Thomas putting his hand in the wound in Christ's side. The third and last panel on the cross shaft shows Christ in glory. He sits on a throne beneath which the devil is shown : the enemy who has been made His footstool. Two figures on either side are thought to be St. Peter and St. Paul. Paul is being given a book, in token of the mandate to preach the Gospel, and Peter is being presented with a sceptre to indicate his primacy.

Above these panels comes the central picture of the Crucifixion. Longinus with his spear is on one side and the soldier who offered

Christ drink on the other. Meantime, two angels support the head of Christ. On the arms of the cross, the pictures are more doubtful, but perhaps show the Ascension and the soldiers who guarded the tomb. Above the Crucifixion is Moses praying during the contest between Israel and Amalek, with Aaron and Hur holding up his hands. This Old Testament event was regarded by the Celtic Church not only as a foreshadowing of the Crucifixion but as a reference to their own pet attitude of prayer : the cross vigil or vigil of the cross, in which one stood with arms extended in the form of the cross.

The opposite face of Muiredach's cross leads up to the Last Judgment. At the base is the Fall, Adam and Eve with the serpent shown coiled round the tree. Alongside, the murder of Abel by Cain is depicted, a type of Christ in that it shows the slaughter of an innocent victim. Above comes David and Goliath, and then Moses smiting the Rock in the desert. The Rock again is the type of Christ : if any man thirst let him come to Me and drink. In the Monasterboice carving, two rows of Israelites queue up with drinking horns in front of the rock. Above, the Old Testament prefigurings are abandoned for the full revelation of the Gospel and the Epiphany is shown, Mary seated with her Child and the Wise Men approaching. On the head of the cross the end of the world's history is shown in a magnificent representation of the Last Judgment ; set on the top of the cross above it, St. Anthony and St. Paul are shown with the bread, that is the type of the Eucharist, coming down from heaven for them. On the sides of the cross, with the ornamental panels, some more pictures are shown, Anthony and Paul meeting, the Flagellation of Christ, Pilate washing his hands and a design that may be intended for the Flight into Egypt.

Muiredach's cross then presents a nicely balanced summary of Christian history. If we are inclined still to shy off from the strange concepts of the Resurrection, first of Christ, and then of ourselves at the Last Judgment, and at the idea of hell ; it is worth remembering that these ideas were just as hard to believe in the first days of Christian preaching as they are today. Science, by working out its details, has not made the decay of a human body any more obvious ; to dip into the writings of the early Fathers of the Church is to find the problem, of how this body can ever be reconstituted at the world's end, frankly stated and discussed, just as they also take up the problem of the mercy of God and the eternal fate of the damned. Against the obvious objections to a physical resurrection of ourselves must be set the almighty power of God, Who, in the first instance, created all things from nothing, and the fact that we make no bones about accepting the idea in reverse. That is, we never think about the miracle that takes place when plant or beast or human baby comes into being : inanimate particles from the earth built up into a living structure. Undoubtedly, this same living structure will rot again into the earth from which it came, but that is no reason that the power of the Lord should not bring it back into being once more.

The Last Judgment of the Muiredach cross is a magnificent piece of carving. Christ stands in the centre holding a cross in one hand and a flowering sceptre in the other. This flowering sceptre may be linked up with the flowering rod of Aaron in the Old Testament. Above Him is a bird, which it has been suggested may be the phoenix, the symbol of Resurrection, though equally it may stand for the Holy Spirit. An angel blows the last trump, and below Christ, St. Michael is shown weighing souls and at the same time thrusting his spear in the mouth of a demon who is trying to upset the balance. On the one hand of Christ are shown the company of the blessed, they are singing and there is a group of musicians to lead them. A bird is perched on one man's harp, as if to give him inspiration. On the other side, the damned are driven into hell by the devil brandishing a trident. Three angels shown above Christ hold a book, which would seem to be the Book of Judgment.

The ideas of heaven and hell were constantly in the minds of the Celtic peoples, and their literature is full of stories about them. That is not surprising, most people do look where they are going, and tend to keep their attention on their objective. The Christian objective is God and heaven.

In Celtic literature, the old pagan stories of adventurous voyages were taken over into the Christian context of the adventures of a saint. In the most famous of these romances, the Voyage of St. Brendan, many of the islands that he visits are not of this world, but belong to heaven or to hell. Later, a vision literature as such came into being, in which the seer, as Dante was to do later, perhaps influenced by the older Irish models, traversed the country of the damned, of those in Purgatory and even ventured to the gates of heaven.

We may find the vision literature crude in its inventions of tortures for the damned, but if we then deny the fact of possible damnation for ourselves, it is because we have forgotten what mercy and justice really stand for. To us, the two concepts stand opposed : we think of mercy as softness, even as letting a man alone to go his own way, whilst justice to us still appears armed with a sword. To try and realise that God is both Justice and Mercy seems to us an impossible paradox, and we like, for our own comfort, to imagine Him merely as merciful ; merciful in the sense that He will let us alone to please ourselves and then overlook all we have done. But that would contradict justice and contradict the teaching of the Cross.

Only in the Cross can we come to some faint inkling of how justice and mercy may be merged. It is the most infinite mercy and love that brought God down to earth incarnate to suffer and to die for us. But it is also the most awful justice, that this sacrifice should be needed to make full reparation for our sins to an offended Deity.

St. Augustine was well aware of this feeling that God will damn nobody. He saw it as another variant of the devil's wiles in Eden. In Paradise, he had persuaded Eve that death would not come even if God was disobeyed ; here on earth, Satan tries to convince us, often most successfully, that it is not possible that God would damn such multitudes and save perhaps only a few. But the evidence for eternal happiness is the same as that for eternal damnation : you cannot believe Christ when He promises heaven and disbelieve Him when He threatens hell. If we doubt the eternity of damnation, we must also doubt the eternity of blessedness.

There exists an Irish poem on the Day of Judgment, which may date back to the 10th century and which forms a literary counterpart to the carvings of the same subject on the high crosses. It begins :—

> "Doom. Not slight will be its uproar when the world will burn ;
> it were meet O Christ with grades (of angels) that Adam's seed
> should dread it."

It describes the separation of the good from the bad, with a sly cut at the Irish lawyers (the brehons) and at the satirical poets who were much hated and feared in a country that loved poetry and in which satire could spread like wildfire.

> "The humble, lowly, devout folk with purity of heart, the
> despised wretches will be in the ranks of heaven's king.
> "The red-mouthed brehons, the lewd, the sinful, the satirists, the
> contentious arrogant clerics will find neither honour nor welcome."

The torments of hell are deftly indicated :—

> "Sorry will be the outcry they will make, dreadful will be their
> wailings, as they part from holy angels, as they go with black
> demons.

"Woe to the soul which heeds not the din of the mighty Day of Doom ; worse seventy-seven times to dwell in hard avenging hell.

"Its bitter cold, its great burning, its hunger, its dreadful thirst, its crushing, its heavy revenge, its horror, its stifling smoke, its slaying.

"Its many fearful monsters, its gnawing, its wild woeful lament, its fiery rotten sea, its vile devilish faces.

God the Father and God the Son are implored for their aid :—

"Of Thy fondness, O fond Father, of Thy gentleness, O king of heaven, cast me not into the bitter prison in which there are many groans."

"For the sake of Thy Cross, of Thy Passion, of Thy Kingship, O Prince, come valiantly to my aid in all the sufferings of my soul."

"Of Thy vast mercy protect me at all times ; put into my soul Thy great love, that it may be overflowing with love for Thee."

Love and mercy were well to the fore in the Irish literature about heaven and hell. In the Brendan Voyage, even Judas is granted an interlude for his sufferings on account of the few good deeds he had done and is released from torment on Sundays and feast days, including the Purification and Assumption of Our Lady.

To return to Monasterboice, and the other great cross, tall, slender and much weathered. Not at all its carvings can be made out, but on one side is the Crucifixion, with Christ mocked on one side of it and the Kiss of Judas on the other, and below, the panels include the Baptism of Christ and the Resurrection, showing the soldiers guarding the tomb. The other side pictures the theme of the help of God rather closely, beginning with David and the lion, then Abraham sacrificing Isaac, Moses striking the rock, David and Goliath, a panel doubtfully identified as Elias mounting the chariot, and finally, on the top of the shaft, the three children in the fiery furnace. Two men heap faggots onto the flames, below which crouch the children protected by the wings of an angel.

On the head of this side of the cross, the principal picture is the Ascension, above is a scene thought to be the appearance of the risen Christ by the sea of Galilee. The Ascension as the central theme of a high cross is unusual, and in this picture the idea of the Christian as a soldier is stressed, for Christ is dressed as a warrior, Who had defeated

death, with sword and shield, and the accompanying eleven apostles
are similarly armed.

It might be tedious to go on detailing the pictures of the high crosses,
or the way in which their ideas were developed and systematized from
the earliest and crudest examples to the later crosses like Muiredach's.
The Old Testament pictures, in addition to those already noted, include
Noah and the Ark—the symbol of the Church and the election of the
just; Adam naming the animals; Abraham and Melchisedech; Moses
receiving the Law; David playing the harp and Jonah being thrown
into the sea. The New Testament pictures give a complete outline of
the life of Christ, much as do the mysteries of the Rosary. So there is
the Annunciation, Visitation, the Presentation in the Temple, as well
as the adoration of the Magi and the message to the shepherds. The
miracle of the wine at Cana and the Baptism of Christ, the miracle of
the loaves and fishes, the three Marys greeted by the angel on Easter
morning; meantime, at Castledermot and Kells, St. Peter is shown being
crucified head downwards. In addition, St. Anthony and St. Paul are
frequently found and other pictures relating to the local Celtic saint
and his miracles and monastery.

If the carvings of the Crucifixion and the Last Judgment may tend
to make us afraid of the justice of God : and St. Gregory in his "Morals"
pointed out that we may well be most afraid of those faults of which
we are not conscious ourselves, that we cannot avoid sin and guilt
altogether, so that even the things that we have done well are not
entirely free from fault if they are judged without mercy; the other
pictures from the life of Christ may give us hope. For this is no distant
God in a far-off heaven that the Christian prays to, but Christ Who
has shared our manhood and our human experience and our problems,
like us in all but sin. The King of Heaven is also the babe in Mary's arms.

St. Augustine's two books about the methods of teaching the Faith,
De Catechizandis Rudibus (The First Catechetical Instruction) and *De
Doctrina Christiana* (Of Christian Doctrine), were known and used in
the Irish monastic schools. In the first, he gives two model instructions,
and from the longer of the two I take a quotation that aptly points
the moral of the carvings of the high crosses, and, in all likelihood,
was used to explain them to the people.

St. Augustine, then, speaks of Christ He "hungered Who feeds all,
He thirsted by Whom all drink is created, He Who is spiritually both
the bread of them that hunger, and the well spring of them that thirst;
He was wearied with earthly journeying Who has made Himself the

way to heaven for us; He became as it were one dumb and deaf in the presence of His revilers, through Whom the dumb spoke and the deaf heard, He was bound Who has freed men from the bonds of their infirmities; He was scourged Who drove out from men's bodies the scourges of all pains; He was crucified Who put an end to our torments; He died Who raised the dead to life. But He also rose again, nevermore to die, that none might learn from Him so to despise death as though destined never to live hereafter."

In that quotation, the high cross patterns begin to twist themselves into a new meaning, and as we study the series of pictures, the fore-shadowings of the Old Testament begin to slide into place and the water from the rock and the manna from heaven take on deeper, mystical meanings in addition to their obvious historical ones. The way in which the panels are arranged brings out how each incident from scripture contains three different meanings:—its obvious historical one, the story of something that happened in the past and added to it; a foreshadowing of the Incarnation of Christ that was to come, for example, the sacrifice of Isaac; and also a meaning for us here and now, not only did God save the children from the fire of the furnace, but He will also, if we ask Him, save us from the fires of our own vices.

In other words, it is a view of history that is geared to one vital date, to the Incarnation of Christ and to His Crucifixion and Resurrection. When the Irish historians tried to synchronise the Irish traditions with world history and particularly with scriptural history, they had a right idea at the back of their minds even if they only succeeded in falsifying their own national history by forcing it into a mould which they had insufficient information to make it fit. The idea was that the whole pattern and meaning of human life on this earth revolves round the Cross.

Whether or not you believe, it must be admitted that this point of view gives a meaning and a purpose both to history in general and the individual's life in particular, which it previously lacked. Man is no longer wandering about in the dark by himself, but following in the track of the pillar of fire across the desert to the Land of Promise. God is not only in command of all events and able to bring good out of evil, but He cares for men, a love reaching to the death on the cross for their redemption. To that essential act, human history led up to in the long ages before the Incarnation, and now for us who come after it, the course and current of events has been transformed, redeemed, the grace of God let loose upon us like a stream in spate. What use we make of that tremendous power is for ourselves to choose, to make the spoon or spoil the horn, in the words of the old Scots' proverb, but our acts are not indifferent and the end of the world will be the signal for the strict judgment of each and all.

This, then, is the message of the high crosses, which still stand, dark and solid against the shifting, storm-driven clouds of the sky, on the Celtic church sites, a view of history set within the framework of the Cross. In this sign not only shall you conquer, but you shall also begin to understand the pattern of life and of world events.

Chapter Nine

SIGN AND SYMBOL

T HE high cross pictures naturally lead us back to the scriptures themselves, and the high cross use of signs and symbols to the exploration of these things in the written word from which they are taken. Already, we have seen the artists of the high crosses using actual historical events like the sacrifice of Isaac to prophecy things to come—the Crucifixion, or to help us in our own problems here and now, our troubles equally subject to the power and control of God as the lions in the den with Daniel. But, in addition, the high cross artists used a few symbols as such :—the lamb to stand for Christ (Kells), the dove for the Holy Spirit (for example, at Clonmacnoise), the hand of God, the symbol of the Creator on Muiredach's cross, the ship of the Church on the Bantry pillar stone, and the vine that stands for the Mystical Body of Christ upon both Muiredach's cross and that at Duleek. Another source for this kind of symbolism was the book of beasts and their legends, the Bestiary. So here at Duleek is a griffin, which was said to live in the desert and carry off large animals as prey—the symbol of the devil ; and, at Tybroughney, the stag which was supposed to trample upon snakes—the symbol of Christ trampling on the devil or of the Christian in his conflict with the world. Drumcliff has a curious cat-like creature which may be the Bestiary Panther. The panther also stood for Christ because it was said to be loved by all animals except the dragon which hated it—the type of the devil.

Our modern reaction to this kind of thing, to the search for hidden meanings and symbols beneath the plain statement of events, is to turn indignantly away from what appears a childish fancy that we have outgrown. The panther is the panther, no more, no less ; the spade, the spade. But is the panther simply panther, sleek and elegant, slipping through the jungle shadows, or could its graceful beauty lead us on beyond the mere anatomy of the beast ? If we insist on calling spades spades and no more, we shut the door upon the whole of poetry, which would read into them the symbol of man's adventure with the earth, of those first cultivations long ago, and of the present conflict between man's need for food and the farmer's ability to grow it.

There seems indeed to be a case for looking twice at things, not merely to assess them in the terms of science, but to feel the pulse and throb of life ; to see the poet's world as well as that of the scientist.

Aileran the Wise, who died in Ireland in the plague of 665, wrote the "Interpretatio mystica progenitorum domini Jesu Christi," in which, working apparently from St. Jerome's "Book of Hebrew Names," he compiled a treatise giving the mystical significance of the geneology of Christ. I single out this example because it would seem to us today about the high spot of the madness of mystical and symbolic interpretation of scripture, to make a book out of a list of names. But it is typical of the attitude of the Celtic Church, indeed of all the Fathers of the Church ; the scriptures are the inspired word of God and, as such, are, as St. Gregory wrote, like a river that is both shallow and deep, wherein both the lamb can find footing and the elephant float at large. There are hidden depths, meanings, senses, to be explored and discovered, and the Celtic Church set itself to work upon them. The study of the Bible, especially the New Testament and the Psalms, was regarded as the highest peak of research. The Irish seem to have been well supplied with Patristic commentaries, and added their own, of which the old Irish treatise on the psalms, already quoted, is a surviving example.

The Leabhar Breac Tract on the Mass includes a passage about the scriptures, which sums up the Irish attitude :—

"One of the noble gifts of the Holy Spirit is the Holy Scriptures, by which all ignorance is enlightened and all worldly afflictions comforted ; by which all spiritual light is kindled ; by which all debility is made strong. For it is through the Holy Scripture that heresy and schism are banished from the Church and all contentions and divisions reconciled. It is in it well-tried counsel and appropriate instruction will be found for every degree in the Church. It is through it the snares of demons, and vices, are banished from every faithful member in the Church. For the divine scripture is the mother and benign nurse of all the faithful who meditate and contemplate it, and who are nurtured by it, until they are the chosen children of God by its advice. For the wisdom, that is the Church, bountifully distributes to her children the variety of her sweetest drink, and the choicest of her spiritual food, by which they are perpetually intoxicated and cheered."

We can set against this Irish account St. Augustine's words in "De Doctrina Christiana" :—

"Scripture asserts nothing but the Catholic Faith, in regard to things past, future and present. It is a narrative of the past, a prophecy of the future, and a description of the present. But all these tend to nourish and strengthen charity, and to overcome and root out lust."

It was with these ideas in mind that the Celtic scholars set about the study of scripture, not indeed in a mood of mere fanciful interpretation or of seeking for things that were not to be found, but bringing to bear all the scholarship that they could make available (and St. Augustine in the book quoted above insists on the basic necessity to do this), and working always in the light of their own faith and love of God. It is always the man who loves God who will understand His word.

But the work of explaining the different meanings of scripture is not, as we tend to imagine, a matter of each individual's own fancy and power of imagination. It is a definite and legitimate field of enquiry with its own fixed rules. Always the starting point must be the ordinary, literal meaning of the words, and then, working from this, one can look for the other meanings that stem from this basic one : foreshadowings of things to come, like the Old Testament figures of Christ, or the miracle of the loaves and fishes, that favourite subject on the high crosses, which foretells the Eucharist; or meanings that apply to our own spiritual life ; or burrowing deeper into the text and finding a fresh meaning by using the words themselves as symbols of other things, as one may take "dog" for example to stand for a preacher. Then too, one may not develop entirely original items of doctrine from these symbols—they only hide what has been clearly stated in other sections of the Bible. The exposition of the text must follow Catholic doctrine and also take heed of the earlier work on the same subject and keep in the track of the commentaries of the Fathers.

Perhaps, today, we feel it is a waste of time to root out meanings in this fashion, when the plain sense is to be found stated elsewhere. Saints like Augustine, and those of the Celtic Church, took the opposite view and found not only the adventure of discovery but a deepening of their own spiritual life as they dug into the mine of scripture. Augustine says in his book on Christian Doctrine that he does not know why exactly but he got a special pleasure from studying the mysteries of the Faith under the various symbols by which they are hidden in the scriptures, and points out that it is often pleasanter to have knowledge communicated in this fashion, and that we get all the more enjoyment from it by having to unravel the meaning. The Holy Spirit, he points out, satisfies our hunger by the plainer passages of scripture and stimulates our appetite by the more obscure.

We may feel that we do not want our appetite stimulated in this fashion, and picking up a book like St. Gregory's commentary on Job, with its wealth of symbolic interpretation, put it down again in disgust. The dog for us is the dog, and not a symbol of anything else. For St. Gregory, the dogs of the flock (Job. 30. 1) stand for the teachers of the Gospel, "which same whilst in behalf of their Lord, they cried aloud, given up to daily and nightly watchings, uttered, so to say, loud barks of preaching."

Yet we cannot cut ourselves off from the use of signs and symbols completely, and if we try to do so completely, we may end in cutting ourselves off from the reality which they represent. Our very knowledge is thirled to signs, for we think and communicate our thoughts to others by the signs of words. There are various kinds of signs, natural ones like smoke that indicates fire, and artificial ones, like words. When one gets to writing, the letters are themselves signs, a sign for the eye of another sign that appeals to the ear. And the word sign may stand for two things, the thing itself, the dog, or the thing that the dog may symbolise, the preacher.

Nor is there really a valid objection to the idea of drawing out further meanings from the symbolism of the scriptures, of starting from the sheep dog and working up to the intellectual concept of the shepherd of the Christian flock. It is only a particular instance of the way our minds normally work, we do start off with sense experience, with the things about us, the dog snapping at our heels, and from these objective things about us, derive the thoughts and concepts of the mind within us.

The way in which such symbolism may be developed comes almost as a shock at first. St. Gregory, for instance, in the commentary on Job refers to the passage in Deuteronomy (24. 6) in which it is laid down that neither the upper nor lower millstone may be taken in pledge—obviously to do so would be to take away a man's means of livelihood. To us, this is merely a bit of legal regulation ; it would never occur to us to use the upper and lower millstones as symbols of hope and fear, and the pledge as confession of sin. Nor would we continue the metaphor as a warning to a reckless preacher neither to rant at the sinner to the extent of making him lose all hope or to go to the opposite extreme and allow him to lose his fear of God.

Again, to us, the cloud in the sky is the cloud in the sky, and a reference to a cloud in the Bible means no more than that. We do not think to ourselves how it can symbolise other things, fickle people who are easily swept away, or the prophets with their hidden wisdom, or apostles and preachers; the showers that come down from the clouds symbolising the rain of their teaching on the dry land of our hearts beneath. The lightnings that flash from the clouds can then be taken as symbols of the miracles of the saints.

Yet to study scripture after this fashion does give a kind of stereoscopic vision to life, the difference between black and white and colour photography. If you have been thinking about looking up to the light of God, the Sun of Righteousness, and seeing the intervening clouds, the saints, just as you may not be able to see the sun itself rising yet see its light on the mountain tops; the sight of the real clouds in the sky filtering the sunset glow onto sea and hillside will take on a new meaning, it will carry your thoughts back to God and the saints by the mere association of ideas, and then, when you return to the scriptural text that brought forth the first idea, the sharp experience of the natural beauty that you saw will come back to deepen the understanding of your reading.

We can to some extent regain this attitude, and come to realise how myths and symbols are not so much useless lumber in the mind, like music and poetry they can convey the mysterious overtones of life that cannot be set out in the plain formulae of scientific speech. Technology as such ousts mystery and leaves us in a coldly aseptic world in which all will eventually be known; the vision of the poet, who deals in symbols and in signs, opens the doors of our hearts to mystery and wonder and beauty, to depths and heights that cannot be plumbed or scaled, but always stretch on beyond our grip, like the vision of the earthly paradise that St. Brendan sought in the voyage legend.

How deeply our lives are penetrated today by an attitude based on scientific technology can be judged by the fact that it is nearly impossible for us to feel any sympathy with, or enthusiasm for, one particular branch of symbolism, that of numbers. The explanations of the symbolism of numbers, scriptural or otherwise, are meaningless to us, though the ancients delighted in them, and if it is legitimate to put a symbolic sense on one item in the Bible, equally it is legitimate to put it on others, like the numbers of particular things. For us, numbers seem only able to mean one thing—mathematical operations geared to our science, and we are quite unable to wrench our ideas loose from this deep-seated attachment and visualise other possible symbols that these figures could indicate.

The Celtic Church, however, suffered no such inhibitions and delighted in the full range of symbolic explanations of the Bible, including the symbolism of colours. Again, colours to us are merely colours, the Old Testament references to twice dyed scarlet will not bring to our minds a symbolic figure of charity, which includes love of God and love of our neighbour under, as it were, the one colour of the virtue. There is a tract on the colours in the Mass vestments in the Leabhar Breac which sets out one interpretation of colour symbols. The priest, says this tract, should withdraw his mind from pride and ambition and reflect on the symbolism of these colours. Gold or yellow stands for the dust to which we must one day return ; blue is humility, our turning from earth to heaven, symbolised by the blue of the sky ; white is purity—the mind white like the foam of the wave, or the swan in the sunshine ; green stands for the earth under which we must be finally buried ; brown is for death and the separation of body and soul. Black indicates penitence, we should shed tears for our sins ; but purple is for the majesty of Christ in heaven ; whilst red stands for His scars and wounds. These explanations of the symbolism of colours are not all exactly alike, but vary with different authors. Something rather similar to the Leabhar Breac tract in idea is St. Gregory the Great's use, in his "Pastoral Care" of the symbolism of the vestments of Aaron which he uses to point out the exemplary conduct that is required of a priest. But he uses gold to stand for wisdom, and whilst still keeping blue as the colour of the sky puts another meaning on it, the need to rise to the love of heavenly things, whilst purple, the royal colour, is used to indicate the need for nobility of spirit.

The Catholic Church can never lose her sense of symbolism, though the degree in which it is explicit in the ordinary Christian's faith may vary enormously from age to age, because her sacraments are themselves signs. The sacraments use sensible things, the water of baptism, the bread and wine of the Mass, both as vehicles of the grace of God conveyed by their means to the soul and as symbols of the meaning and working of that grace. If we are really conscious of the full symbolism of the things used in the sacraments we shall, however, deepen our own spiritual life and awareness, and penetrate further into their mystery.

There is, for example, this matter of the symbolism of water and the symbolism of baptism. In Celtic Ireland and Scotland, this symbolism was particularly appreciated because there had already been a well-established pagan cult of holy wells, which the saints blessed and brought into the new Christian context. Every agricultural people, every nomad with a herd to water, realises something of the symbol of the spring. For him, water stands for life, for the Christian it stands as symbol of the supernatural life, of the grace of the Holy Spirit. The pagan sees the rain fall on the parched land and the grain, buried in the earth, sprout into new life; the Christian sees in baptism the new life of the soul; we, as it were, buried with Christ in the waters of the font, and then rising to a new supernatural existence.

The holy well is a constant accompaniment of the Celtic Church site. It was essential, of course, everybody needs a water supply, but the way in which its cult has persisted to the present day seems not so much a matter of a lingering paganism, as of the Celtic saints stressing the symbolism of water, linking up the old belief with baptism and with their studies in the scriptures.

The way in which these water symbols came to penetrate men's minds is indicated by some passages in the life of St. Senan of Scattery Island, in the Book of Lismore. In this account, the angel Raphael tells the saint, when he founds his church and monastery on Scattery Island in the mouth of the Shannon, that it will become "a head of devotion and a well of wisdom of the West of the World," and at the end of the story, Senan himself is extolled as "the glassy well whereby all the folks which God entrusted to him are washed by the purity of his teaching."

Here then is an obvious instance where the use of the symbol helps us to understand the meaning, the idea of teaching that springs up clean and cleansing from the rocky depths in a ceaseless stream. And this is the whole point of the use of signs and symbols, not to confuse, but to make plain, not to make a mystery but to lead us deeper into the understanding of a mystery. The objective of the Celtic scholars who studied the mystical and symbolic senses of the scriptures was to speak in light what they heard, as it were, in darkness.

So then, we can go back to the carvings on the high crosses and find them full of new meanings and life, a vivid commentary on St. Augustine's statement that in the Old Testament the New is concealed, and that in the New Testament the Old is revealed (in veteri testamento est occultatio novi, in novi testamento est manifestatio veteris). Our own experience will react upon their symbols; the Rock that is Christ and the rock in the desert from which the Israelites obtained their spring of saving drink mingling with the rocks and springs that we ourselves know in a strange cross-fertilisation by which the memory of the symbol brings us back to God, and the thing itself, the water from the cliff, enriches that very symbolism. For, if we have a sense of symbolism, the basic need of the spring for ourselves and our beasts and farms will bring us back to our supernatural need for the grace of God that the water symbolises : symbol and reality will interact and bring about a mysterious integration of material and spiritual worlds.

Or we can go back to the Antiphonary of Bangor and explore its symbols, beginning to appreciate the hymn that most likely was used for the blessing of the Paschal candle, in which the idea of the light as symbol of God leads on, past the pillar of fire that led the Israelites, to the candle itself, the flame standing for the Holy Spirit purifying our bodies represented by the wax, and finally, to the bees that made the wax, ourselves like a new swarm of bees flying up into heaven.

The symbols may be unexpected. One of the surviving certain compositions of St. Columcille is the famous "Altus Prosator," a long Latin hymn, written in alphabetical form, in which the story of the Creation, the Fall of men and angels, the sustaining of the present world by God, and the Last Judgment, are vividly presented. In it, the certain return of the stars, Vesper and Orion, as used as types of Christ, because they disappear and then appear again at a fixed time and place. Yet again, we may be surprised at St. Maelruain of Tallaght having the Song of Songs sung over the dying Céili Dé monk because "in that canticle is signified the union of the Church with every Christian soul."

To return to the Antiphonary of Bangor, there is included in that collection an attractive little song about the merits of the Rule of the monastery of Bangor and the monastic life, which is made up of a pattern of different symbols. The context in which they are used seems more unfamiliar to us than the symbols themselves, which are now more often found applied either to the Church as a whole, or to Our Lady, the type of the Church. Here then are the symbols of the Christian ship in the sea of this world, of the house built on the rock standing firm against the storms that beat on it (and Bangor was on the seashore and knew what it was talking about), the city set on the hill, the fold of Christ, the vine that had been brought out of Egypt, abandoning the pleasures of this world for the desert and the Land of Promise beyond it.

Benchuir bona regula,	Good the Rule of Bangor,
Recta, atque divina,	Correct and divine,
Stricta, sancta, sedula,	Strict, holy, constant,
Summa, justa, ac mira.	Exalted, just and admirable.
Munther Benchuir beata,	Blessed the company of Bangor,
Fide fundata certa,	Founded on certain faith,
Spe salutis ornata,	Graced with the hope of salvation,
Caritate perfecta.	Perfect in love.
Navis nunquam turbata,	A ship never distressed
Quamvis fluctibus tonsa,	No matter how struck by the waves,
Nuptiis quoque parata,	Also prepared for marriage,
Regi Domino sponsa.	A bride for the sovereign Lord.
Domus deliciis plena,	A house full of delights
Super petram constructa,	Built upon the rock,
Necnon vinea vera	Also the true wine
Ex Aegypto transducta.	Brought out of Egypt.
Certe civitas firma	Surely an enduring city
Fortis, atque unita,	Strong and united,
Gloriosa, ac digna,	Glorious and deserving,
Supra montem posita.	Placed upon a hill.
Arca Cherubin tecta,	The ark sheltered by the Cherubim
Omni parte aurata,	Completely covered with gold,
Sacro-sanctis reperta,	Filled with sacred objects
Viris quator portata.	Borne by four men.
Christo regina apta,	A queen fit for Christ,
Solis luce amicta,	Clad in sun light,
Simplex, simulque docta,	Innocent yet wise,
Undecumque invicta.	On all sides unconquerable.
Vere regalis aula,	A truly royal hall
Variis gemmis ornata,	Decorated with many gems.
Gregisque Christi caula	The fold also of Christ's flock
Patre summo servata.	Kept by the supreme Father.

Virgo valde fecunda	A virgin very fruitful
Haec et mater intacta,	Also a mother most chaste,
Laeta ac tremebunda,	Joyful and reverent
Verbo Dei subacta.	Submissive to the word of God.
Cui vita beata	For whom a happy life
Cum perfectis futura,	Is laid up with the perfect,
Deo Patre parata	Prepared by God the Father,
Sine fine mansura.	Ordained to last for ever.
Benchuir bona regula.	Excellent the Rule of Bangor.

The Rule of Bangor went across Europe with Columbanus and across Scotland with Moluag. The Bangor missionaries were faced not only with the real sea to cross, but with the storms of vice and intrigue and violence in the countries in which they founded monasteries and churches. These phrases about a city set on a hill, about a house built on a rock and about purity and innocence and wisdom, about the virgin mother, are not mere words picked out at random, but the symbols of an ideal that the Celtic monks attempted to live up to and to preach to others.

Chapter Ten

THE EARTH IS THE LORD'S

THE first miracle that Ciaran of Saighir, "first born of the saints of Ireland," worked, was, according to the *Life*, when he was a small boy and saw a kite snatch a little bird off her nest. Ciaran made the kite drop the injured prey and, miraculously curing the small bird, restored her to her brood. Later, Ciaran went off to live as a hermit in the woods and the animals were his first monks, the fox and the badger, the boar, the wolf and the doe, all living peacefully together except when the fox nature asserted itself and stole Ciaran's sandles to eat.

Ciaran of Saigher was a real person, quite apart from the truth of the stories about his pet animals, and he was one of the saints of Ireland who introduced Christianity in the south of that country before the coming of Patrick. But the animal stories about the Celtic saints persist through the whole period of the Celtic Church, and form a characteristic section of Celtic hagiography. Pet foxes, deer, cranes, even flies ; wild animals suddenly tame and docile with the saint ; domestic animals behaving miraculously—St. Brigit of Kildare's cows produced incredible amounts of milk and butter ; the list is almost endless.

We can at once pick up some of the threads of the story : in an agricultural country, miracle stories about cows and sheep will always be popular and appreciated, so too will stories in which a wild deer is induced to pull a cart in place of a horse, or like that of St. Abban making wolves act as sheep dogs. But other stories stem from a pure love of animals as such, Columbanus getting the squirrels to come down to him from the trees so that he could pet them, or Moling feeding bread to a pack of hungry dogs, or Columcille nursing up the storm-spent crane that managed to make a landing on Iona. There is here a love for animals like that of St. Francis, and perhaps the very success of the Franciscan movement has obscured its forerunners in this direction.

The Christian who loves animals and has a strange power of handling them did not appear with Francis, but with the desert hermits, with Anthony asking the wild creatures to leave his little plot of garden alone.

With the love of animals goes a love for natural beauty. Again, we connect that Christian realisation of the beauty of nature with Francis, and again we ought to look for its sources far beyond him, in the Psalms and the Fathers of the Church and in Celtic Ireland. The Celtic monks almost always picked the sites for their monasteries not only for utility, land, water, communications, but for beauty. I cannot resist quoting the measured Victorian phrases of the archaeologist, J. Romilly Allen, in this connection :—

"No one who has visited any considerable number of ancient ecclesiastical buildings can fail to have been struck by the care which the monks took in selecting sites where feelings of religious devotion might be intensified by the contemplation of all that is beautiful in nature. Sometimes the church stands beside a brawling stream, amidst the sylvan scenery of some secluded glen ; or it is found by the banks of a broad river flowing through the rich meadows of the plain ; or, as at Aghadoe (outside Killarney, Co. Kerry), the charm lies in the extent of the landscape to be seen from an elevation with its ever-changing effects of light and shade and variations of colour."

Indeed the very names of famous Celtic Church sites conjure up pictures of natural beauty : Iona and Tiree with their flashing sands ; Clonmacnoise, green turf beside the Shannon ; the fantastic rocks of Skellig ; the panorama of sea and mountain circling Inismurray Island ; Gougane Barra, hidden in the mountains by a corrie lake ; and Aghadoe, of which Romilly Allen wrote, commanding the mountains and lakes of Killarney. The very sites themselves proclaim the attitude of the Celtic Church to natural beauty, and its poet saints, like Columcille, sang of it. An Irish poem, almost certainly of Columcille's making, sings of the Iona outlook, the sea and the waves, the sandy beaches, the wheeling birds, the queer creatures of the ocean—whales frequent these waters at times, and of the saint varying his occupations from prayer and contemplation and psalm singing, to giving food to the poor, catching fish and picking dulse (edible seaweed) off the rocks. But there is a subtle difference in this attitude to that of mere appreciation of beauty as such, nor is there the tendency of the pagan lover of nature to make her a goddess and mix the creator and created into a pantheistic whole. For Columcille, the earth is the Lord's :—

> "That I might bless the Lord
> Who conserves all,
> Heaven with its countless bright orders,
> Land, strand and flood."

And he ends :—

> "The King whose servant I am will not let
> Anything deceive me."

All the time the saint is aware of created beauty, he is also aware of uncreated Beauty; the thought of the one leads up to that of the other, but they remain utterly distinct, he pets the squirrel and delights in its tawny fur just because it is the creation of the Lord Whom he loves.

A 9th century Irish poem describes the Celtic ideal of a hermitage, mingling the beauty of nature with the symbolism of water, and setting the whole as background for the little monastic community and for the church in which the Mass is offered :—

> "I wish, O Son of the living God, O ancient, eternal King,
> For a hidden little hut in the wilderness that it may be my dwelling.
>
> An all-grey lithe little lark to be by its side,
> A clear pool to wash away sins through the grace of the Holy Spirit.
>
> Quite near, a beautiful wood around it on every side,
> To nurse many-voiced birds, hiding within its shelter.
>
> A southern aspect for warmth, a little brook across its floor,
> A choice land with many gracious gifts such as be good for every plant.
>
> A few men of sense—we will tell their number—
> Humble and obedient, to pray to the King :—
>
> Four times three, three times four, fit for every need,
> Twice six in the church, both north and south :—

Six pairs beside myself,
Praying for ever the King who makes the sun shine.

A pleasant church and with the linen altar cloth, a dwelling for
    God from Heaven;
Then shining candles above the pure white scriptures.

One house for all to go for the care of the body,
Without ribaldry, without boasting, without thought of evil.

This is the husbandry I would take, I would choose, and will not
    hide it:
Fragrant leek, hens, salmon, trout, bees.

Raiment and food enough for me from the King of fair fame,
And I to be sitting for a while praying God in every place."

There are two tendencies in Christianity, one to mount up to the
Creator by means of His creation, and the other to turn sharply away
from all created good things in order to concentrate upon uncreated
Goodness. And the saint needs to have a bit of each of these apparently
opposed trends, he must not get intangled in created things and miss
the infinitely greater wonder and beauty of their Creator thereby; yet
he must not despise them, as some spiritual writers are a little careless
in suggesting he should, because to do so would be to insult God and
the workmanship of His world. But there is always a tendency to this
latter exaggeration: it seems to have come from the East and from the
Greek philosophies; the feeling that the soul is caged within the body
and not a part of a body/soul unity, and that we need to get completely
clear of matter to contemplate Divinity. To take that idea to an extreme
is to deny Christianity which is based upon the Incarnation, upon God
becoming Man and using our humanity as the road to bring us to His
Divinity. Or, as the Preface for the Christmas Mass puts it, by seeing
God in visible form, we are carried away to the love of invisible things.

The Christian attitude to beauty and to nature and material things
goes back to the creation of the world, to the statement in Genesis that
God created the world and saw that it was good. Evil was not created,
evil and sin came from the rebellion of angel and man created good,
and neither evil nor sin are to be found, therefore, located in matter
as such.

So then, the beauty of the world ought to lead us on to the beauty of the Creator, of which it is only a faint reflection. The 13th chapter of the Book of Wisdom details this idea, and St. Paul, in the first chapter of his epistle to the Romans, uses the same theme, that creatures ought to bring us on to knowledge of God, and not beguile us into making idols of them. If perhaps we had at the backs of our minds the idea that St. Francis discovered the Christian attitude to nature, it comes as a shock to read St. Cyril of Jerusalem's panegyric about the material world, written in the 4th century when he was lecturing his catechumens on God as Creator. Cyril told them how they ought to catch a glimpse of the glory of God in the world He has made, not only in sun and moon and stars, but in the changing shapes of clouds, in the colours of flowers, the knots of the reeds' stems, the fishes in the sea. St. Augustine had the same idea—for him all things were beautiful because God had made them. St. John Chrysostom, commenting on the verse in St. Matthew (6. 28, 29) about the beauty of the lilies of the field, asks "Wherefore then did He make them so beautiful? That He might display His own Wisdom and the excellency of His power; that from everything we might learn His glory."

St. Gregory in the *Morals* speaks of the wonder of nature, why should we wonder at the miracle of Aaron's rod budding, and yet take not a bit of notice at a tree growing or coming into leaf, which is equally wonderful. Nor do we wonder at the rain falling on the vine and being eventually converted into grapes and then into wine, though we wonder at the miracle of water being made into wine in the one sudden stage. And he puts the attitude of the Celtic saints, who read his book, and indeed what ought to be that of all Christians, to nature, rather concisely :—

"If we look attentively at outward things, we are recalled by their very means to inward things. For the wonderful works of the visible creation are the footsteps of our Creator. For we cannot as yet behold Him Himself; but we are yet tending to a sight of Him, if we admire Him in these things which He has made. We call therefore, the creation His footsteps, because we journey onwards towards Him by following up those things which proceed from Him."

He goes on to point out how the soul comes to find God by the very things which drew it away from God before it was converted. St. Gregory says that it is very fitting that we should rise by visible things to invisible ones, thus reversing the order in which we fell. And this is what the Celtic Church did to a high perfection ; they were not drawn away from God by natural beauty, but brought closer to Him by it.

It is a startling experience to see the world for the first time as something that God has created, and it brings about a sudden and deep reverence for everything ; one is almost afraid to touch the petals of the flowers or stroke the rock with its tufts of lichen. It is the kind of awe that goes with a master craftsman putting a very beautiful and delicate piece of workmanship into your hands.

But, and this is vital, you cannot snatch at these things for your very own. For the earth is the Lord's, and not only did He create it, but He keeps it in being ; you cannot separate a created thing from the power of God which maintains the thing's very existence. And from that comes the realisation that you can never really own anything in the sense of having complete dominion and control over it, it belongs in the full sense to God and you only have the use and the enjoyment of it.

It could be that present-day feelings against the dogmas of the general bodily resurrection, and of the assumption of Our Lady, are tied up with our lack of appreciation of God as creator and sustainer of the world. We tend to take scandal at Catholic Christianity because it is so tied down to material things, this woman and this man, these sacraments, and to think that a purely spiritual religion should be our proper objective. It seems that this desire for a belief that is not thirled to things or to history may be linked up with our ordinary human desire to eat our cake and have it—we would like to have the comfort of belief in a rather distant God and we would also like to have material things for our very own. The Christian God is not distant and un-interested, He became Man, and the Christian dogma insists that we must not set out hearts on making a cairn of treasure in this world to have for ourselves.

So then, the Celtic saints managed both to delight in the world—for who would not delight in something that their own Beloved had made ? —and kept themselves from becoming tangled in it, from seeing no further than the thing itself and not looking beyond it to its Creator. The attitude gave a very delicate and graceful touch to their writings and their work ; the Irish scribe could look up from copying and scribble in the margin :—

"A hedge of trees surrounds me : a blackbird's lay sings to me—
      praise which I will not hide—

above my booklet the lined one the trilling of the bird sings to me.
In a grey mantle the cuckoo's beautiful chant sings to me from
   the tops of bushes:

May the Lord protect me from Doom! I write well under the
   greenwood."

Those lines come from the St. Gall Priscian, an MS. probably copied
in Ireland in the 9th century and later taken to Europe by the Irish
monks.

In the Codex Sancti Pauli, from the monastery of St. Paul in Carinthia,
another 8th or 9th century Irish MS., is the famous poem about the
student and his white cat, Pangur: the student hunting words and
wisdom and Pangur hunting mice. In the Martyrology of Tallaght
(contemporary with that of Oengus the Culdee) there are little bits of
natural history linked up with the saints' days and written in the margin
of the Latin text. They are in Irish. For Ciaran of Clonmacnoise,
September 9, there is, for instance, the note:—"On the festival of
Ciaran, son of the wright, wild geese come over the cold sea."

It is interesting to trace the stories about animals from the desert
hermits through St. Martin to the Celtic saints. Sulpicious Severus, in
his "Dialogues" about St. Martin, gives first an account of the desert
hermits and tells some stories about them, and then goes on to parallel
their exploits with his own hero, St. Martin. So the story goes of one
hermit who had a pet wolf that came each day at mealtime and was fed
with scraps of bread. One day the hermit was visited by another monk
and, going to see the latter part of the way home, was away when the
she-wolf came for her dinner. The animal snuffled round the empty cell
and eventually found out the hermit's basket of bread, from which she
helped herself. Returning, the hermit found a loaf missing and guessed
what had happened. The wolf meantime did not reappear, knowing she
had done wrong. The hermit looked for her and prayed for her return,
and, at last, after a week, she came, in a very hang-dog attitude, asking
to be forgiven. The hermit petted her and gave her a double ration of
bread, and the two returned to their old footing of friendship.

Coming to St. Martin, the tradition of the saint's friendship with
beasts is continued. Martin meets with a savage cow and realises that
it was being driven wild by a demon riding on its back. He told the
demon to let the innocent creature alone, and the cow, relieved from
its tormentor, came quietly to the saint and lay down at his feet. In

another story, Martin rescued a hare from a party of hunters and their dogs ; at his command the hounds stood still as if chained to the ground, whilst the hare fled away into safety.

Pagan Ireland already had a love of nature and many folk-lore stories about animals ; with this ancient tradition the new Christian one mingled, and blossomed forth in the immense animal literature about the Celtic saints. Much of it is inevitably pure romance and miracle, but the basis is in the reality of the Celtic saints' love for all creation and delight in the diversity of animal and plant.

Just as Martin could halt the dogs, so the traditions tell of the Celtic saints keeping herds within certain bounds that they marked out for them with their croziers, so that they should not stray. St. Columbanus is said to have been worried by a bear robbing his orchard, he, like St. Anthony in the desert, interviewed the bear and told it that it could have certain trees for its own use and must leave the rest alone for the monks.

There are many stories about bees, for honey was an important foodstuff. One beautiful little story tells how a priest lost the Host whilst carrying it on a journey and the bees found it. They set to work and made a tabernacle and church and model priests all in wax, and placed the Host there for safety. Meantime, the priest was very distressed and did penance for a year, at the end of which he was brought to the bees' wax church and recovered the Host.

St. Patrick is said, when he began to build his new church at Armagh, to have found a deer and its fawn on the site. The men with him wanted to kill it, but Patrick would not allow this and took up the fawn in his arms and carried it off to another hill nearby where it could be left in safety.

The list could be continued almost indefinitely, from wonder stories like that of the bees and the Host, to probabilities like Patrick and the fawn. But they all lead back to this basic attitude of the Celtic saints to animals and nature, and the use of their interest and delightfulness and beauty as a kind of ladder leading up toward God. The mind does not rest in created things, but looks beyond them and breaks out into praise of their Creator. Columcille in the *Altus Prosator* brought out this point in his description of the creation. He tells of God making heaven and earth, sea and waters, the blades of grass, the twigs of shrubs, the sun and the moon and the stars, the birds and the fish and the cattle, and finally, man himself. As soon as the stars were made, Columcille says the angels broke out in praise of God for the wonder of His creation. That idea, of course, continues in the *Benedicite, omnia opera Domini Domino* of the three children in the fiery furnace, the whole of creation being called upon to praise the God Who made them. That canticle, which is included in the Antiphonary of Bangor, must have been kept well to the fore in the people's minds by the very frequency of the carvings of the children on the high crosses.

But there was probably a deeper level in this love of nature of the Celtic Church. Nobody can sing the psalms or read the Bible without to some extent appreciating their references to natural beauty, to mountain and spring and torrent, but equally, one can be led to a sense of their symbolism of other spiritual realities. The Celtic saint, who had so often herded cattle in his youth, would so very readily pass from the watching of the sheep stringing out over the Irish hillside, to the scriptural symbols, the good shepherd leading out his flock onto the mountain pastures and letting them drink at the fountain of living water—the grace of the Holy Ghost. And if he, like Patrick on Croagh Patrick or Brendan on Mount Brandon or Assicus on Slieve League, built himself a hermitage on the top of a mountain, he would not only appreciate the ever-changing pattern of sea and mountain and field set out below him, but would also be constantly brought back to the scriptural symbolism of mountains.

For the hermit on the heights, when the mist swept down upon the tops, he could not but be reminded of the cloud on Sinai and Moses, or of the Transfiguration of Christ. Christ Himself had gone off up the mountain to pray, and the Celtic saints followed in His track, realising, as they did so, that His action meant more than a mere hill climb, that it symbolised the need of every Christian to go apart and pray in the solitude of the high places.

The mountain symbol is interwoven through the scriptures, and the Celtic saints would be quick to catch the different meanings : the mountain standing for Christ, or for the Church, or for preachers, and so on. The picture in Psalm 103, of the Lord sending rain upon the hills, would bring them at once to the idea of Christian teachers and preachers raised up like mountains and receiving the rain of wisdom to pass on to the lowlands of ordinary people. Or again, they might think of the mountain symbolising Christ Himself in the clean beauty of the rocky heights, the summit from which all the meaning and pattern of the world below can be discovered.

Yet again, there is the constant idea of the spiritual life as an ascent, from the valley of humility up to God. We are back with Moses on

Sinai, we scramble up the heights of prayer as best we can and God stoops down from heaven to meet us, as it were, half-way.

There were deer running wild on the Irish hills in the period of the Celtic Church, just as they run wild on the Scottish mountains today, stepping elegantly over the grass and springing easily amongst the rocks and across the streams. The stag, its hooves clattering on the bare rock as it passed the Celtic hermitage, might well bring to mind another aspect of the mountain symbol—the deer as standing for the Christian, moving in nimble bounds up to the heights of contemplation (Psalm 17 uses this symbolism, v. 34, where God is said to have made the singer's feet like those of the deer and brought him out onto the heights). As the stag moves off the rock and lowers its head to crop the grass in the corry, the Celtic saints may have thought of the Christian feeding on the teachings of the apostles and preachers that the mountains symbolise and from them gaining strength to go bounding over the summit ridges.

Certainly, Celtic Ireland knew the deer well, and the stories of the saints tell of their friendship with them—the tame doe that milks herself into a stone basin for the benefit of one of the saints being a recurrent hagiographical theme.

There is another aspect to the symbolism of the mountain and to the Celtic hermitages on the heights : there is a price to be paid for the freedom of the hills, the ascent has a penitential side to it. There is a renunciation of the comfortable things of this world, the snugness of the glen and the fireside, the shelter of the wood and the ease of smooth walking, for the rock and the sting of wind-driven hail—and the splendour of the beauty of the summits. It is the paradox of Christianity that you must, as it were, abandon and leave behind the lowlands of this world in order to climb out onto the heights, but when you have gained the ridge, the country beneath can be seen, and enjoyed, for what is really is, for the first time. And this is perhaps the key to the attitude of the Celtic saints to nature, the man on the mountain top, joined to God in the cloud of contemplation, but yet able to look back, down the sudden drop of the precipice and the smooth grassy slopes of the hillside, to the world beneath, the sparkling sea, the sand of the beaches, the checker-board of little fields, the dark gashes of the peat cuttings, the smoke rising from the cottage chimneys, and take delight in all these things without becoming lost and mazed amongst them. The man on the low ground may be confused and bewildered, even lost, amongst the trees or the bogs or the fields ; the mountaineer is seeing the whole of the picture.

Chapter Eleven

PENANCE AND PILGRIMAGE

ST. COLUMBANUS said that, just as one ought to pray each day, so one should fast every day too. Bangor lived that teaching, the monks only having the one meal in the evening all the year round. If we turn away from the idea, and from the more exotic stories about Celtic penance in the "Lives" of the saints (which have lost nothing in the telling), as something indicative of the wild enthusiasm of the Celtic past, we miss the whole point of Columbanus' thought, which is, that penance ought to be as much a regular part of the Christian's daily life as prayer.

Legends apart, Celtic penance was severe. We know a good deal about it from the little handbooks of sins and the appropriate penances which the Celtic Church compiled. Those books, and the customs and teaching of the Celtic Church seem to have influenced the Catholic Church as a whole : the systematic lists and their commutations helping the development of indulgences, and the Celtic insistence on frequent private confession and penance as against the long public penitential routine of the early Church, helping to make that the normal Catholic custom. The Celtic idea was that just as a room gets brushed out every day, so should one's soul by very frequent confession, not only of serious sins, but of the small venial ones too—these small things mount up just as the small drops of rain built up the rivers into spate.

We get a dramatic picture of the Celtic saints : of their fasts and vigils, of standing in lake or sea or river to recite the psalms, of praying in cross-vigil, with arms extended in the form of the cross. They were very much in earnest, the second-best would not do, it must be a total effort for the Lord. The same spirit is abroad always, but the way it shows itself depends on where the particular individual's treasure is ; he may go on an all-out effort for the kingdom of heaven or he may make the same sacrifices to climb Everest or break speed records or make scientific discoveries.

The first objective of Celtic penance, of any penance and asceticism, was the attack on the individual's own sins, to make reparation for them, and to get the body and soul back into a proper state of health, so that the passions can be kept in control by the reason and the will. It is, of course, obvious that the sense of sin and of its hatefulness will increase with the individual's own sanctity : the nearer you are to God the more conscious you are of your own failings and fallings short, just as bright sunlight will show up small defects in something that appears perfect in dimmer illumination. But that leads on to a much more positive attitude to penance. Charity drives us on not only to be concerned for other people's sins, but to try and do something about them, we are all linked up in the Mystical Body of Christ, and the saint can take effective action therefore on behalf of other people. There is the insistent urge to make reparation to God for the rest of the world's sins. And from that the emphasis shifts again, to join Christ in His sufferings, the Man Who was really completely free from sin and Who suffered and died that we might live. The Christian must cling to Christ, and that means clinging to the cross ; he must want to prove his love for God to the point of dying for Him. The logical conclusion of the Christian life is martyrdom.

But the opportunity to lay down one's life for Christ is not always and everywhere available, and the Celtic saints, in a country whose conversion needed no martyrs, tried to make up for that lack by penance and austerity. From that came the phrase "white" martyrdom for severe penance, as against the "red" martyrdom of death for the Faith. Actually, that idea had begun to appear in the desert : St. Athanansius speaks of St. Anthony's life as a kind of martyrdom, he had escaped death during the persecutions when he went to help those who were executed or imprisoned, but his own life in the desert to which he returned thereafter was a sort of martyrdom. The idea becomes quite explicit in Sulpicius Severus' writings about St. Martin of Tours, who, he says, would have welcomed the opportunity if the times had allowed it, but who by his own life had gained the same glory as the martyr. It is the theory of the Celtic Penitentials system of commutations : you could exchange a long penance for something shorter and sharper ; you could reach the same end by the long drawn-out struggle of asceticism and penance as by the short one of persecution and death.

There is a rather fascinating fragment of an Irish homily upon this subject, written in alternating Latin and Irish as is so often the case, and dating from the second half of the 7th or the early 8th centuries. It was a stray fragment that a scribe had got mixed in with the text of the *Collection Canonum Hibernensis* that he was copying, and, somewhat uncritically, included in the middle of his proper text. From the place where the MS. has been preserved, this fragment goes by the name of the Cambrai Homily. It begins by speaking about the need for penance :—

> "Si quis vult post me venire, abneget semet ipsum et tolat crucem suam, et sequatur me. This is the word which our Lord Jesus saith to everyone of the race of men, that he banish from him his vices and his sins, and that he gather virtues and receive stigmata and signs of the Cross for Christ's sake, so as he is in power of body and soul, that he follow the tracks of our Lord in good thoughts. Therefore he says : Si quis vult post me venire abneget semet ipsum et tollat crucem suam, and let him take up his cross, et sequatur me, and let him follow me. This is our denial of ourselves, if we do not indulge our desires and if we abjure our sins. This is our taking-up of our cross upon us, if we receive loss and martyrdom and suffering for Christ's sake."

The homily goes on to refer to the Mystical Body :—"if there be any little ailment on a man's body, if it burns a place, whether in his foot or in his hand or in his fingers, the disease inflames the whole body. Thus it is fitting for us ourselves, that every suffering and every ailment that is on his neighbours should inflame every part, for we all are members under God as saith apostulus : quis scandalizatur et ego non uror ? quis infirmatur et ego non infirmor ?" This leads straight on to the matter of martyrdom :—

> "The holy apostle has said this from the abundance of his charity ; everyone's sickness was sickness to him, offence to anyone was offence to him, everyone's infirmity was infirmity to him. Even so it is meet for everyone of us that he suffer with everyone in his hardship and in his poverty and in his infirmity. We see in these wise words of the sage that fellow-suffering is counted as a kind of cross. Now there are three kinds of martyrdom which are counted as a cross to man, that is to say ; white martyrdom, and green martyrdom, and red martyrdom. This is the white martyrdom to man, when he separates for sake of God from everything he loves, although he suffers fasting or labour thereat. This is the green martyrdom to him, when by means of them

(fasting and labour) he separates from his desires, or suffers toil in penance and repentance. This is the red martyrdom to him, endurance of a cross or destruction for Christ's sake, as has happened to the apostles in the persecution of the wicked and in teaching the law of God.

"These three kinds of martyrdom are comprised in the carnal ones who resort to good repentance, who separate from their desires, who pour forth their blood in fasting and in labour for Christ's sake."

The green martyrdom of the homily seems to have been used for the canonical penance imposed on people who had committed grave sins, and probably deriving from this, on pilgrimage over seas "for the love of Christ" or as an imposed penance. The great type of the ideal of white martyrdom was, very naturally, Job in the Old Testament, but St. Martin must have been a more immediate source of inspiration. Martin's death has about it, the authentic flavour of Celtic penance. Sulpicius writes :—

"For several days he was in a high fever, yet he never ceased to worship God. All night in prayers and watchings he forced his weakening frame to serve the spirit, lying in sackcloth and ashes. When his disciples begged him at least to allow some common bedding to be placed beneath him, he said : 'It is not seemly for a Christian to die save on ashes :—if I leave you any other example, I have sinned'."

They begged him to allow them to give him some relief by turning him on his side, and he refused even this—St. Ciaran of Clonmacnoise dying on the turf outside his new church there was to say the same to his monks who wanted to move him off a sharp stone on which he was lying. "He that endures to the end shall be saved," said Ciaran.

So too, the "Rule of Columcille," which seems to be a 9th century composition for the use of hermits living attached to a neighbouring monastic centre, speaks of the need to have "A mind prepared for red martyrdom. A mind fortified and steadfast for white martyrdom."

There is an Irish homily on the subject of repentance in the Leabhar Breac. It says that it is necessary to do penance both for sins actually committed and for the good that we might have done but did not. There are three ways, says the homily, in which sins can be forgiven, baptism, martyrdom, penance. There is a much more detailed list in the Penitential of Cummean (c. 650) which gives twelve different ways

by which sins can be remitted. This list seems to have been taken by
Cummean from a homily of Caesarius of Arles, who in his turn got
it from Cassian's conference with Abbot Pinufius. Cassian did not
originate the idea, but seems to have been working from the list of
seven remissions given by Origen in his "Second Homily on Leviticus."
By such devious and distant routes did ideas come to the Celtic Church
to be put into action. Cummean's list begins with baptism and ends
with martyrdom. The items in between are, however, on a different
footing : they are things that we can do, or have done for us, to make
reparation for our sins. The confession mentioned in the middle of the
list is not apparently ordinary sacramental confession, the Christian's
normal method for getting his post-baptismal sins remitted, but a general
admission of one's sins :—the scriptural reference given is to Psalm 31,
v. 5, 6, "I have acknowledged my sin unto thee (God) . . . and thou
hast forgiven the wickedness of my sin."

Cummean's list is :—baptism ; charity (this refers to Luke 7. 47 in
which Christ told the woman weeping at His feet which she anointed
that her sins were forgiven, pointing out that she had also greatly
loved) ; alms-giving ; the shedding of tears ; confession ; affliction of
heart and body ; renunciation of vices ; intercession of saints ; the merit
of mercy and faith ; the conversion and salvation of others ; our own
pardon and remission of other people's injuries to ourselves—"forgive
and ye shall be forgiven" ; and martyrdom.

Finnian's Penitential (c. 525-50), probably St. Finnian of Clonard,
which Columbanus made use of in compiling his Penitential, says how
it is necessary to eradicate sins from our hearts by the help of God
and our own energetic activity, and proposes a method of proceeding
by contraries, to cast out the vice and replace it by the appropriate
virtue. Patience must replace wrath ; charity, envy ; liberality, greed ;
spiritual joy, dejection ; and so on. The Celtic saints may have sometimes carried things to an extreme, but these writings are not extremist,
they are very level-headed common sense. You cannot root something
out and leave a gap, and the thing that will best fill the gap left by
some habitual vice is its contrary virtue.

Perhaps one of the most striking items of Celtic writing on the
subject of penance is the so-called "Litany of Confession." It is attributed
to a St. Ciaran, probably meaning Ciaran of Clonmacnoise, but it is
actually much later in date than his period, though it may have
originated from his foundation of Clonmacnoise. It begins by invoking
the Trinity and then calls upon God by a very beautiful series of titles :—

King above all kings, Cause above all causes, High-priest of all creation, and so on, and then in striking terms details the effects of sins upon the penitent :—

> "Come to help me, for the multitude of my inveterate sins have
>   made dense my too guilty heart ;
> They have bent me, perverted me, have blinded me, have twisted
>   and withered me ;
> They have clung to me, have pained me, have moved me, have
>   filled me ;
> They have humbled me, exhausted me, they have subdued me,
>   possessed me, cast me down ;
> They have befooled me, drowned me, deceived me and troubled
>   me ;
> They have torn me and chased me ;
> They have bound me, have ravaged me, have crucified me, rebuked
>   me, sold me, searched me, mocked me ;
> They have maddened me, bewitched me, betrayed me, delayed me,
>   killed me.
>   Forgive."

Reverting to the litany of titles of God, the invocations move majestically forward with the cry "Forgive" inserted at intervals :— O guiding light, O holy Narrator, holy Scholar, O overflowing, loving silent One. Then God is begged to take action against sins :—

> Propter nomen tuum Domine, propiciaberis peccato meo.
> Many and vast are my sins in their mass, through my heart and
>   round about it like a net or a breast-plate ;
> O King, they cannot be numbered ;
> Despoil me of them, O God ;
> Break, smite and war against them ;
> Ravage, bend and wither them ;
> Take away, repel, destroy them ;
> Arise, scatter, defeat them ;
> See, repress, waste them ;
> Destroy, summon, starve them ;
> Prostrate, burn, mangle them ;
> Kill, slay and ruin them ;
> Torture, divide and purify them ;

Tear, expel and raze them;
Remove, scatter and cleave them;
Subdue, exhaust, and lay them low.
Heavy then and bitter is
The subdual and the piercing;
The bond and the fetter;
The confusion and the maddening;
The disturbance and the raging;
     which the multitude of my sins brings upon me.

Then the litany asks the forgiveness of God by all the various actions of the Incarnation, the womb and paps of Mary, by everyone who saw or touched Christ and by Our Lord's own patience, humility, uniqueness, nobleness by the passion and the Resurrection and Ascension:—

"By every creature whereon the Holy Spirit came, from the beginning of the world to the end;

By Thy coming again the day of doom; (grant) that I may be righteous and perfect, without great dead on me of hell or doom, without soreness or bitterness on Thy part towards me, O Lord;

For my sins are blazing through me and around me, at me and towards me, above me and below me.

Alas, Alas, Alas, forgive me, O God.

Every sin which I did, and took pleasure in doing;

Every sin which I did under compulsion, or not under compulsion;
    Forgive.

Every sin which I sought after, or did not seek after;
    Forgive.

Every evil that I did to anyone, or that anyone did to me;
    Forgive.

Every evil wherein any one took part, or did not take part with me;
    Forgive.

Everything which I sought for, or did not seek for; found or did not find;
    Forgive me.

Everyone to whom I did good unjustly, or evil justly;
    Forgive.

Every good which I did and marred; every evil which I did, and
did not make good;

> Forgive.

Every provocation which I gave to God or man;

> Forgive me.

Every sitting down, every standing up; every movement, every
stillness; every sleep, every sleeplessness; every forgetfulness,
every remembrance; every carelessness, every carefulness;
every longing, every desire, every lust; every thought, every
love, every hate, which is, which was, which shall be mine,
to my life's end.

> Forgive me.

Every will, every displeasure, which I have harboured against God
or man;

> Forgive me.

Every ill that I did, every good that I omitted, every sin within
sin, every ill within good, every good within ill that I did.

> Forgive me for them. Amen.

The length and detail of the litany of Confession is typical of Irish
devotion of Celtic times, a liking to explore into everything, but there
is also an alert watchfulness about it, a determination to let nothing be
slurred over in this examination of conscience.

The ideas linked in the mind of the Celtic Church with that of
penance were those of the Christian soldier and of martyrdom; of action
positive and adventurous, of struggle with our own sins and with the
devil. It is the attitude of mind reflected in the prayer in the Roman
Missal after the imposition of ashes on Ash Wednesday, which refers
to the fast begun that day as the defences of the Christian army—we
who are going to fight against spiritual wickedness are to be strengthened
by self-denial. Or to quote an Irish source, there is the Second Vision
of Adamnan, which seems to date from the 11th century, and was
written to command the people of Ireland to fast to avert a pestilence
which it was feared might come upon the country. It says that:—

> "It is through fasting and prayer that the kindreds of men have
> been brought from the devil's power, after Christ had been forty
> days and nights, drinkless, foodless, fighting with the devil on
> behalf of Adam's children. And it is out of compassion that Christ
> did that, so that fasting and prayer should be every human being's

chief harbour against every distress that may come to them from heaven or earth."

Fasting, says the Vision, is always an indestructible rampart against destruction, a straight path to heaven, a renewal of friendship with God and an increase of penitence and charity in the heart. Small wonder that Columbanus said that we ought to fast each day just as we pray daily; the soldier is not going to lay aside one of his most effective weapons in the heat of the battle.

Celtic penance leads on to Celtic pilgrimage. The Celtic monks were great travellers—pilgrimage was said to be part of the Irish nature. They went to the Holy Land and to Rome, to visit the shrines there, they went over Europe and Britain, preaching, teaching, studying, founding monasteries. Some went for the sheer delight of adventure and travel, but there was a penitential aspect to Celtic pilgrimages : the "exile for the love of Christ," the man who left his country and his own people to go and preach in a foreign land, as Columbanus did, vowing never to return home again. And again, for serious crimes, pilgrimage for a period or permanently, could be imposed as a penance.

The "Life of Columcille" in the Book of Lismore writes at length about the idea of pilgrimage as introduction to Columcille's own life work in Scotland. Three kinds of pilgrimage there are, says the "Life," leaving one's country for love of God, and forsaking vice for virtue ; leaving one's country in body only and with no change of heart, and for this no reward is got of God, for it is by practising virtue and not mere motion of the feet that will bring us to heaven ; and the third kind of pilgrimage, the man who longs to go but cannot because of his duties at home, whose good will will have the same value as the journey and exile that he could not undertake. The Leabhar Breac homily on repentance stresses the pilgrimage idea too, it says that there ought to be a change of place in doing penance. Peter denied Christ at Jerusalem and did penance for his sins preaching amongst the many nations of the world ; Adam was cast out of Eden. "Everyone today who does penance should follow in their footsteps" and go away from the place where he sinned to another to do penance.

Two concepts are mingled here :—the first, the giving up of home and kindred for the love of Christ, the "Life of Columcille" quotes the example of Abraham ; and the second, the whole of life seen as a pilgrimage, of which our own small pilgrimages, temporary or permanent, are the symbolic figure.

Only perhaps at rare intervals do we see our lives as a pilgrimage, as something very transitory passing across the stage of the world. But watch the crowd in the city streets, all men under sentence of death, the town itself almost a permanent thing through which this stream of men is moving, being born, growing up, dying ; coming into the world, travelling through it and passing out of it again. We cannot settle ourselves down here and now for good and all, for this is no permanent home of ours, we are all travellers on the road, going somewhere, heaven or hell, but shifting, moving always in the flux of life.

This idea was constantly in the Celtic saints' minds, the adventurous journey through the world, a journey to a definite objective, but an objective not certain of attainment. The issue would remain in doubt until the very end, as it should in all the best adventures ; the traveller might go astray or be waylaid by brigands. He could enjoy the country through which he passed, but he must not try and settle down in it, or look back to the homeland of his birth that he had abandoned— the road to the hills lay ahead and needed all his attention and energy if the peaks were to be gained.

But the road that the Christian follows is essentially in the track of Christ, the Celtic pilgrimage through life has all the austerity about it of the taking up of the cross and an unflinching and uncompromising following of Jesus to the bitter end. The cross-vigil, that favourite attitude of the Celtic monks in prayer, is symbolic of their whole outlook. The cross vigil was widespread in the early days of the Church, St. Maximus of Turin, who died soon after 465, says that prayer offered in this position will be more quickly answered, because the body imitates the Crucified whilst the soul speaks to Him. The imitation of Christ is laid upon all Christians, but the emphasis may shift from age to age— the Celtic Church seems to have put its stress fairly and squarely upon the imitation of the Passion. Columbanus said that true penance was to avoid doing the things for which penance was necessary, to avoid sin. This avoidance of sin is the beginning of the imitation of Christ : it led men like Columbanus on to a life of penance that was wholly positive in its outlook and direction, the total offering of themselves to God of the martyrs, the carrying of the cross with Jesus like Simon of Cyrene.

There are no limits to love. The man in love will lay down his life for his friend joyfully, almost glad to have the opportunity of proving the depth of his devotion. The urgent problem of the saints is just that, how to give to God some token of their love for Him, some answer to His infinity of love for us. Christ Himself left no room for doubt of what following Him, keeping close to Him, would entail—the taking of the cross. Neither the Celtic saints, nor those of other times and places have shrunk from that challenge and command. If we today are inclined to shrug off that ideal of penance and asceticism as, at best, a religious eccentricity; it may be linked up with our lack of love for God—we do not spare ourselves in effort or endeavour or endurance when we are going after something that we really want.

Chapter Twelve

THE LIGHT IN THE ISLANDS

FROM the mountain ridges of Mull in the Inner Hebrides, the climber looks down upon the sea inlet of the Firth of Lorne; beyond it the mountains rising in a mighty line, the massive Nevis, the horned crests of Cruachan. Set in the sea, dark and lumpy masses of rock, are the tiny Garvellach Islands, craggy and hard to land upon, but lush and fertile withal in the shelter of their cliffs. On Eileach an Naoimh, "the Rock of the Saint," the ruins still stand of a Celtic monastery, the heather growing in thick tufts upon the top of the wall of the ruined beehive vaulted oratory. It seems reasonable to hold that Eileach an Naoimh is the "Hinba" of St. Adamnan's biography of St. Columcille; that the old chapel with its garland of ling is either the very one, or built upon the site of that in which Columcille offered the Mass of the Saints, assisted by Sts. Comgall, Brendan of Clonfert, Kenneth and Cormac, when St. Brendan saw a globe of fire over Columcille's head at the consecration.

Hinba was something of a hermitage, something of a penitential station. It lay within an easy sail of Iona, and was also on the shipping route from Ireland; its original founder seems to have been Brendan, but it later passed into the hands of Columcille and Iona. To it, Columcille seems to have come often enough; it must have been a much quieter retreat than Iona for prayer in its rocky isolation, yet it was not entirely cut off from the world and the saint could keep in touch with any urgent developments.

On Hinba, according to Adamnan's account, some of the most striking occasions of St. Columcille's prayer were manifested. Not only the globe of fire blazing up into a bright pillar at the Mass of the Saints, but other times: three days and nights when Columcille was rapt in prayer in his cell, neither eating nor drinking, and, again, circled by a mysterious brilliance of light. Afterwards, St. Columcille said that during this period of contemplation, many things, including some difficult passages of scripture, had been made plain to him. The weather was wild at the time and Colum's foster-son, Baithene, to whom he longed to confide a full account of his experience, was storm-stayed upon the island of Eigg.

The prayer of the saints seems, according to a persistant and often well authenticated tradition, to be sometimes accompanied by this strange brilliance—it was reported of Columcille upon Iona as well as on Hinba, and of other Celtic saints. But the point at issue is not so much the light as what it signified, that Columcille and others of the Celtic saints seem to have experienced the highest levels of contemplative prayer, and further that they combined this sort of prayer with a life of often violent activity in the world. On Hinba, Columcille, aided, says Adamnan, by a vision, decided the political future of the infant Gaelic kingdom of Scottish Dalriada and determined who should be its next king. With Columcille you never feel very far removed from the stress and turmoil of events, from the conflict between the Scottish Picts and the Irish settlers of Dalriada, from the complex pattern of Irish politics and rivalries, or from the government of the great chain of Columban monasteries in Ireland and western Scotland. Yet it is this same man, who seems to have a controlling finger in every pie, who lands upon the little Hinba and spends three days and nights in an ecstasy of contemplative prayer. I quote the example of Columcille, because his biographer, Adamnan, lived near enough the saint's time to be a reasonably reliable source; but the same impression exists of many other Celtic saints, they nearly always seem to have combined the active and contemplative ideals that we tend to think of as separate ways of life. Some were permanent hermits indeed but more often, the hermitage was a temporary retreat, a springboard for fresh endeavour; the light that shone on Hinba and Iona was a beacon light for the coasts of all the countries round about. *Contemplata aliis tradere,* the fruits of contemplation and of the knowledge and love of God must be brought to others, the Celtic saint was not merely enlightened himself but set out to bring that light to the rest of the world.

What was a saint like Columcille like to meet as an individual? Adamnan gives some account:—he calls him an "island soldier" of Christ, a man who from infancy had lived dedicated to God, preserving purity of soul and body, so that even "on earth he was fitted for a heavenly life." He was "clean in speech, holy in deed, of excellent disposition, great in counsel"; constantly engaged in work of some kind, prayer, reading, writing, manual labour, fasts and vigils that seemed beyond an ordinary man's endurance. Throughout, he always showed a "pleasant, holy countenance, he was gladdened in his inmost heart by the joy of the Holy Spirit." There were other things about Columcille, too, a handiness with boats, a certain obstinacy and a flash of very Irish temper, the vision of a poet mingled with that of the man of prayer and added to a great capacity for leadership and negotiation. A dangerous man to cross; but if you had his friendship, you could trust it to the world's end.

The very sharp division between the active and contemplative ways of life seems to go back to Origen, who was the first to explain the Gospel account of Martha and Mary as symbols of the two sorts of activity. The division is, of course, well justified; it is, to a large extent, the divide between earth and heaven. In heaven, we shall be occupied with contemplation of God, with the beatific vision; here, on earth, we are engaged in the job of reaching that objective, with fighting down our sins and vices and cultivating the virtues and with all the variety of things that concern our relations with and love of our neighbour. Yet the division between the two ways of life is not clean cut; we cannot in this life see God face to face, but yet we can here and now make a beginning on the life of heaven; Columcille on Hinba in the darkness of prayer gaining some experimental knowledge of his Lord. Eternal life, the life of heaven, is essentially a matter of knowing and loving God, and that we can, in the night of faith, begin to do here and now, indeed we must do so, to be Christian at all. Christ Himself has told us that the man who eats His flesh and drinks His Blood already has eternal life; if we want to study Celtic prayer, we are brought back to Celtic devotion to the Mass, and to that dramatic pre-figuring of it in the Old Testament, of Elias exhausted and starving in the desert revived by the heaven-sent bread and able to walk to Mount Horeb, the symbol of the summit of perfection.

Perhaps it is easier to think about the active and contemplative lives in the terms of that little-known writer, Julianus Pomerius. Pomerius had been born in Africa but eventually came to settle in Gaul, where he was the teacher of St. Caesarius of Arles. His surviving book, *De vita contemplativa*, "The Contemplative Life," was written at the end of the 5th or the beginning of the 6th centuries. It is concerned with the active and contemplative lives and with the virtues and vices and it is directed to bishops and clerics, not to hermits or groups of contemplatives cut off from the world. The bishop ought, and here Pomerius' model example is St. Augustine, to combine contemplation and action, his prayer spilling over into and directing all his work for souls. So Pomerius puts the distinction between the two ways of life rather differently from that of modern writers, it is not a matter so much of a way of life as a state of soul, the active life is that of the soul seeking for perfection ; the contemplative life that of the soul which has reached or is reaching perfection. Seen under these terms, Columcille the politician and Columcille the mystic are no longer contradictories.

So St. Gregory in the *Morals* nicely sums up the Celtic ideal, which, after all, is really nothing more than the literal and exact following of Christ. For Christ "in the daytime exhibits His miracles in cities, and spends the night in devotion to prayer upon the mountain, namely, that He may teach all perfect preachers, that they should neither wholly leave the active life, from love of the speculative, nor wholly slight the joys of contemplation from excess in working, but in quiet imbibe by contemplation what in employment they may pour back to their neighbours by word of mouth. For by contemplation they rise into the love of God, but by preaching they return back to the service of their neighbour." It is easy to show the Celtic saints carrying this ideal out— St. Columbanus travelling the roads of Europe, and getting a she bear to give up her cave to him for a hermitage for prayer and penance to which he could retreat ; St. Patrick leaving the cares of the young Church in Ireland to spend a Lent upon the summit of Croagh Patrick ; or St. Brendan dreaming and scheming of adventure on the high seas from a mountain oratory. Out of the swirling mists of the hills, St. Gregory made a symbol of this kind of life, the saints caught up like water by the heat of the sun, to contemplate God and then descending from this prayer at the icy crests, like snow to water the earth with their teaching and example.

The whole organisation of the Celtic Church was geared to this kind of life. It was almost entirely monastic, but the monks did not live shut within their monastic enclosure ; they served the congregations round them, and undertook immense and extensive missions to Europe and Scotland, as well as travelling for study or on pilgrimage as such. The monastic organisation was largely centralised : Columcille controlled all his string of foundations in Ireland and Scotland from Iona, and this seems to have been the usual grouping, a series of monasteries dependent on the chief church of the founder saint.

But they did not launch out on their widespread activities without due preparation. They imitated Christ, Whose life indicates very pointedly that the enthusiast should not rush wildly forth to preach to others the moment the urge to do so strikes him. For the public life and preaching of Jesus was preceded by the fast and temptations in the desert: we can hardly expect to go by an easier road. The man who would teach must not only know what he is to teach but understand it in the light of long hours of prayer; he must not preach only by words but by example, he must first learn how to be a good Christian himself. Adamnan's words about Columcille being "trained as an island soldier" refer to something very real—the Celtic monk, before being sent out to teach Europe, had a long training in asceticism and prayer. The very fact of their far reaching and adventurous apostolate explains something of the harshness of the Celtic standard of penance. The monk who lives enclosed in his monastery all his days needs a much less rigorous training than the monk who is going to venture out into the rough and tumble of the world and who must keep his head in every sort of stress and strain and how to behave in any situation, from a king's court to a melee with a band of robbers. It is the difference between the training of the regular soldier and the training of the commando. In fact, Adamnan's "island soldier" phrase does indicate the kind of man the Celtic monastery trained up; the impression is of the small boat running in on the rocky island, the crew disciplined and skilful and ready for anything.

The basis of Celtic prayer, the road that brought the saints to the highest levels of contemplation, and gave them the driving force to travel the roads of the Western World, preaching and teaching, is very simple. It can be ours for the taking. The background is ascetic, penitential, and without let-up. Penance is as normal and continual as prayer. It is for the individual to decide what he can and cannot do— the Celtic Church was careful to consider the particular man's capabilities and capacity—but as Cassian's desert hermits were quick to point out, everybody can do something. But prayer and penance interlock; the climber to the heights, the soldier, must go into some sort of training if they are to reach their objectives.

Celtic prayer as such stemmed from the Mass and the liturgy and from the study of scripture. There is a marked emphasis upon study, the "Rule of the Céili Dé" says that the kingdom of heaven is granted to him who directs study, him who studies and him who supports the student. From studying the scriptures and thinking about them, and the Celtic monks seem to have had the psalms off by heart, it is a very short step to thinking about God and praying to Him. With their day patterned by the liturgy, with a deep realisation of its symbolism, with the phrases of the psalms stored in the memory, the Celtic monks were led to a continual awareness of God, of the angels and the saints. This sense of the supernatural coupled with a set purpose to serve God must inevitably lead the individual closer and closer to God and to His love, and out into the high places of prayer.

It is usually advisable to seek guidance and advice before scaling the heights, however, and the Celtic Church laid great emphasis on the necessity for everyone to have a "soul friend," a confessor and director to guide them in the spiritual life. So the 8th century "Rule of Comgall" says :—"A devout sage to guide thee, 'tis good to avoid punishment. Though great thou dream thy firmness, be not under thine own guidance." In selecting such a soul friend, St. Maelruain of Tallaght advised to "seek out the fire that you think will burn you the fiercest."

The old Irish Rules set out some of the ideals of the Celtic monk : learning, steadiness, humility, patience, penance. So the Rule of Comgall :—

> "This is the essence of the Rule : love Christ, hate wealth ; piety
> to thee toward the king of the sun and smoothness toward men.
> "Continuance in penitence—wonderful the road, keenness,
> persistence there in : heed of death every day ; good will to every
> man."

And the Rule of Ailbe :—

> "Let him be steady without a particle of weakness ; let him be
> an anvil for every profitable thing ; let him perform the desire of
> every person ; let him answer the sins of every soul.
> "Let him be gentle, close and zealous ; let him be modest,
> generous and gracious ; against the torrent of the world let him
> be watchful, against the brood of the world let him be warlike."

The Rule of Carthage, which is thought to belong to the beginning of the 9th century is divided into sections dealing with the needs of the different classes of the Christian community, bishops, monks, Céili Dé, and so on. In it, the ideal of the abbot like Columbanus or Columcille, who is also an apostle, is set out and linked up with the Mass—the abbot's ideal is to be "continual preaching of the Gospel to instruct all, offering of the body of the Great God on the holy altar." The same ideals are set out at much greater length by non-Celtic writers, St. Augustine in "De Doctrina Christiana" had indicated what a Christian preacher ought to be like, and how he ought to vary his technique according to his audience and win their love and sympathy. So too, later, St. Gregory in his "Pastoral Care" gives a picture of the ideal ruler and teacher of the Christian flock, the man who lords it over vices rather than subjects, a man who can be stern when the necessity demands it but to whom the people can turn in their troubles as to their mother. The Celtic preachers, at their best, came up to that ideal, very humble, very capable, very sympathetic, but utterly unbending toward sin. There is a charm about them that goes with St. Gregory's statement that the seed of the word will only germinate properly in the listener's heart if it is watered by the kindness of the preacher ; the Celtic saint was a lovable individual.

He was also a very determined individual ; determined in prayer as well as in his relations with his fellow men. He not only did not give up the attempt to pray because it did not come easily, but forced conclusions with heaven. The hagiographers give a gloriously comic account of the Irish saints literally haggling with God and refusing to take "No" for an answer. Perhaps one of the best stories is of Patrick on Croagh Patrick engaged in a typically Irish bit of hard bargaining with an angel, and eventually getting his own way. The old account tells of his going to Croagh Patrick "to do violence to heaven until his petitions were granted" and so they were, even to Patrick's getting the right to judge the people of Ireland at Doom. The angel told Patrick that he was the most excellent man that had appeared since the Apostles, save for his obstinacy. That story is Irish fun and love of haggling, but it does indicate an underlying reality : that prayer was, for the Celtic saints, as for everyone sometime or other, something hard and un-yielding, a matter of persistence and "doing violence" not only to oneself by penance but also to heaven by a refusal to be discouraged and to give up.

The outcome was the holiness of a man like Columcille, gladdened always "in his inmost heart by the joy of the Holy Spirit." So too, in the old story of St. Brendan and St. Brigit, Brendan telling Brigit that since he had been ordained he had never gone over seven ridges without his mind turning to God, and Brigit's devastating answer, the answer of the contemplative, "By the Son of the Virgin, from the time that I set my mind on Him, I have never taken it from Him."

This permanent awareness of the indwelling of the Trinity in the soul, of the nearness and love of God, is contemplation, but in Brigit it meant also action. The oldest accounts give an impression of no cloistered nun but a woman continually "on the road" in her chariot, her activities ranging from converting pagans to the Faith to those of the modern agricultural adviser. She knew about cows and sheep and how to manage them, she knew about men and women and how to deal with them too; the Kildare convent was a base for a roving apostolate in the country round about.

The Celtic panegyrics of St. Brigit may be taken as one of the ideals of the Celtic Church, of the woman saint. Her proudest title is the "Mary of the Gael," she was regarded as a person who modelled very closely Mary's perfection, so much so that she could be thought of almost as Mary. The "Life" in the Book of Lismore extols Brigit's virtues, her kindness to the poor, her modesty, gentleness, humility. "She was abstinent, she was innocent, she was prayerful, she was patient: she was glad in God's commandments: she was firm, she was humble, she was forgiving, she was loving: she was a consecrated casket for keeping Christ's Body and His Blood: she was a temple of God. Her heart and her mind were a throne of rest for the Holy Ghost."

St. Patrick himself can hardly be taken as typical of the Irish and Scottish Celtic saints, he was British, and the adventures of his youth and his captures by the Irish raiders meant that he never had the opportunity to cultivate the kind of learning that was normal in the later Celtic Church. Yet again, he does conform to their pattern of life, the man of deep prayer who is also a man of action, and St. Secundinus' hymn about him does present the kind of ideal that the Celtic saints lived.

This hymn, *Audite omnes*, is included in the Antiphonary of Bangor and is always attributed to the St. Secundinus who was one of the bishops sent to help Patrick in his Irish mission. It seems quite probable that he did write the hymn, and that it is a truthful picture of Patrick; its terms indicate that the saint was alive when the hymn was composed. It is in the favourite alphabetical form of the Irish writers, each verse beginning with successive letters of the alphabet. The hymn begins by asking us to listen to the merits of Patrick, who is like the angels in goodness and equal to the apostles because of his perfect life.

> Audite omnes amantes Deum sancta mereta
> Viri in Christo beati Patrici episcopi,
> Quomodo bonum ob actum similatur angelis
> Perfectamque propter vitam aequatur apostolis.

The theme is the apostolate of Patrick linked with his good works and good example; he is God's faithful servant and His ambassador, his preaching is both in words and in deeds. The Cross in which Patrick glories, is his sole comfort, his body is a temple of the Holy Ghost, he is the Gospel candlestick shining over the earth, and the fortress of the King set upon the mountain. This man will be greatest in the kingdom of heaven says the hymn, who fulfils with his good deeds the things that he preaches. The hymn then speaks of Patrick's love of the scriptures and his belief in the Incarnation of Christ and in the Trinity; Patrick sings the psalms, the Apocalypse and hymns, explaining their meaning to the people, his own prayer is unceasing. His reward in heaven will be to reign with the Apostles.

The stress then falls upon going in the track of the Apostles; this was the ideal of the Celtic preacher and missionary. It was an ideal, the literal following of Christ and the life of the Apostles, that was abroad at a later period of history, the inspiration of the Dominican and Franciscan Orders just as of the Celtic Church. Perhaps we are inclined to miss the point and see only the acceptance of the Gospel poverty and the wandering preacher rather than look to the source of energy of his activity and renunciation. That is, it is easy to visualise Patrick and the possibly mythical shamrock, and the Irish crowd, but not so easy to come to grips with Patrick's own prayer and contact with God in the Irish solitude. It is easy to read the Acts of the Apostles as a kind of travelogue, without understanding that the flames of Pentecost were not mere publicity for the infant Church, but signs of a deeper, spiritual fire within each Apostle himself.

Look again, and you see with the Celtic saints that every Christian ought to go in the track of Peter. If I have stressed Celtic activity, it is not because the Celtic saints did not realise that the real initiative always remained with God. It was Christ that called Peter from his fishing; it is He Who chooses each of us too, we who deny and fall short of our calling. Nor can we by our own efforts gain the beatific vision of heaven, or its obscure beginning in prayer here and now; it is something that must be given us by God, like the fire of Pentecost and the coming of the Holy Spirit. But if the highest levels of contemplative prayer are something infused, something given; their result is not passivity. The disciple is moving very close to Christ, trying to model himself on Him, to reach St. Paul's dramatic claim of "not I but Christ living in me," and Christ is the good shepherd, tramping after the strayed sheep on weary feet. The apostle's charity is the mainspring of his action, his love of and union with God, and his love of his neighbour in whom he sees Christ—the twice-dyed scarlet thread of the Old Testament. According to John Cassian, this apostolic love is the normal outcome of the attempt to live a really Christian life. How that comes about was neatly summarised for him by one of the desert fathers, the Abbot Pinufius. He said that the "beginning of our salvation and of wisdom is, according to scripture, 'the fear of the Lord.' From the fear of the Lord arises salutary compunction. From compunction of heart springs renunciation, i.e., nakedness and contempt of all possessions. From nakedness is begotten humility; from humility the mortification of desires. Through mortification of desires all faults are extirpated and decay. By driving out faults virtues shoot up and increase. By the budding of virtues purity of heart is gained. By purity of heart the perfection of apostolic love is acquired."

This was the route that was followed out by the Celtic monks. There is a striking little story and poem, very Irish in its phrases and symbols, in the Book of Leinster, which gives a slightly different angle on the same subject. It indicates first of all the very simple things that went to make the Celtic saint, the serving of God in all things, study, penance, and then breaks into a vivid description of the qualities of such a man.

The Book of Leinster then tells how once the devil appeared to St. Moling as a prince and told the saint that he was Christ. Moling would not believe him, for said he, "Christ always appears to the Céili Dé as a sick man or a leper." The devil admitted his identity but asked the saint's blessing and Moling refused, saying it would be of no use to him. So the devil asked for the "full of a curse." Moling asked why he wanted a curse and the devil said, "Not hard to say, O cleric, the mouth whereon would come the curse on me, its hurt and poison shall be on thy lips." "Go," answered Moling, "you deserve no blessing.' The devil, however, suggested that he could earn a blessing, and asked Moling how he could do so. "Service unto God," answered the saint. "Woe is me, I bear not this," said the devil. "A little even of reading." "No more of reading, it helps me not." "Fasting then." "I am fasting from the world's beginning. Not the better am I." "Prostration to make." "I cannot bend forward, for backwards are my knees." "Go forth," said Moling, "I cannot teach or save you."

"He is pure gold, he is a heaven round the sun,
    He is a vessel of silver, full of wine,
    He is an angel, he is wisdom of saints
    Everyone who doth the will of the King.

He is a bird round which a trap shuts,
He is a leaky bark in dangerous peril,
He is an empty vessel, he is a withered tree,
Whoso doth not the will of the King.

He is a sweet branch, with its blossom,
He is a vessel which is full of honey,
He is a precious stone with goodness
Whoso doth the will of God's Son of heaven.

He is a blind nut, wherein is no profit,
He is a stinking rottenness, he is a withered tree,
He is a wild apple branch without blossom,
Everyone who doth not the will of the King.

If he does the will of God's Son of heaven,
He is a brilliant sun round which is summer,
He is the image of God in heaven,
He is a vessel glassy pure.

He is a racehorse over a smooth plain,
That man who strives for the kingdom of great God,
He is a chariot that is seen under a King,
Which wins a prize from bridles of gold.

He is a son that warms holy heaven,
The man for whom the great King is thankful,
He is a temple, prosperous, noble,
He is a holy shrine, which gold accompanies.

He is an altar whereon wine is shed,
Round which is chanted a multitude of choruses,
He is a cleansed chalice with liquor,
He is white *findruine*, he is gold."

Chapter Thirteen

ISLAND OF SAINTS

THE children, as like as not, will follow you if you go through the farmyard and across the fields to the grass-grown ramparts of the old fort, and remain quietly watching, fingers in mouths. A group of straggly pines on the bank top, the bracken in the ditch below shoulder high; the temptation is easy to fall for, the feeling that the world of the Celtic fort was totally other than ours today. Yet if anything is certain at all, it is that the children from the simple little huts within the fort would have come running out after the strangers, just as they have come out now from the farm house new built in concrete blocks. Man can change his environment, increase his material comforts, but he cannot change his own essential nature.

It is that we should remember at any ancient site; not let the sense of otherness, of strangeness, lead us away from the essential fact that the men who once lived and died here were of the same kind, of the same loves and passions and ambitions as ourselves. The grassy banks of the old Celtic fort where once lived a colony of skilled metal workers, the round tower and the high crosses of the Celtic monastic site, the faint outlines of the royal palace of Tara, the ruined beehive cell in the field wall, the massive ramparts of the great stone forts; it is easy enough to think that these things belonged to a people quite different from ourselves, and for that assumption to imagine a golden age, a time when Ireland was a land of saints and scholars.

Undoubtedly, the history of the world has its ups and downs—civilisations and cultures come and go—and the Ireland of the Celtic Church, and the adjacent Celtic lands of Wales and Scotland, were on a peak of Celtic culture. Ireland's schools did attract scholars from all the Western World, the fame of her saints was likewise widespread, and there is indeed the impression that the Celtic countries then

133

possessed more than their fair share of saints. But if Celtic Ireland's interest centred very largely upon the monasteries and on the idea of holiness; if this period of history was marked by a strong tendency to take Christianity seriously; it does not follow that it was any easier to be a saint in those days and that the Celtic saints found life straightforward enough. It seems very possible that they found it excessively hard, for the devil is always on the prowl to attack goodness; it is the man who is trying to cling to God on whom he will concentrate his efforts, the mediocre and the bad are his, or almost his, already. Temptations, the struggle with evil within oneself and in the world round one; these things were part of the Celtic pattern of life just as much as the idyllic picture conjured up by the title of "Island of Saints and Scholars."

Our modern scientific studies inevitably tend to make us concentrate always on the latest discovery, and then to imagine by a kind of analogy, that we, the discoverers, are the latest sort of men and that our experience is new and cut off from that of men of past and less scientifically enlightened ages. The educated man of today no longer reads the classics—if he did, it might be with the same kind of shock that one gets when first beginning to read the Fathers of the Church: finding that these men were just as intelligent, just as much alive to reality as ourselves, and that their problems, though in a different material setting, were much the same as our own.

If then, the patristic literature that Celtic Ireland studied shows a deeper insight into the minds of men and their behaviour than the writings of our modern psychologists, who tend to study part rather the whole of man's nature, and if the history of their times shows the same familiar recurrences of evil and sin, then we can no longer think of the Celtic saints as remote, an academic study. They were men like ourselves, with the same passions and the same difficulties.

We must, however, note one great difference between the world then and the world today. Now, Western Europe has largely lost its sense of belief in God; it no longer thinks of God as a factor in everyday life that must be taken into account. This disbelief in God, or in a set of gods, is not the normal condition of the human race—the past took religion and the idea of God seriously as something that must be considered in one's daily life. Yet, even so, the gap between the saint and the man who accepts the existence of God and maybe goes to church on a Sunday, is enormous, just as is the gap between the really good pagan and the ordinary one with a back-of-the-mind belief in the pagan pantheon. Just because all our knowledge starts with our senses and with material objects, we have a basic tendency to materialism, in fact, even if not in the particular philosophy of the age in which we happen to be born. It is always hard to think of the world as made up of spiritual and material realities and harder still to live that belief. Even in Celtic Ireland, a country taking its new found Christianity very seriously, there is no evidence to suggest that it was excessively easy to turn to God. It was so much easier to concentrate on the here and now: the cow that one could haggle over and covet rather than on the invisible Holy Spirit. Only the terms have changed—the cow was the currency unit in Celtic Ireland just as the pound and the dollar are ours today. For most of us, even if we pay lip service to the Cross and the view of life and reality that it implies, the cow and the dollar are the real objects of our efforts and affection. A fast chariot, a fast car; a new house, a new stone fort; a string of pearls or the Tara brooch—there is always something here and now to put in the place of God and to draw our attention back to the earth and to material things.

So then, we ought to view the achievement of Celtic sanctity against the difficulties of Celtic times. In the small states into which Ireland was divided, pride and ambition and petty wars were always liable to break out. Even the monasteries were involved in these clannish groupings; not only attached in loyalty to the local kinglet, but sometimes in trouble with him. St. Carthage (Mo-chuta) had established a large and flourishing monastery at Rahan. Mo-chuta came from Munster and many of his monks likewise, and Rahan lay on the border between the territory of the Munster Eoghanacht and the Ui Neill. There was trouble between the two peoples, for Munster was trying to encroach on the Ui Neill; it was perhaps very human, but hardly to the credit of the title of "Island of Saints," that the Ui Neill evicted Mo-chuta and his monks and that they had to trek south to a new foundation at Lismore. In Scotland, there seems to have been little love lost between the churchmen of the Pictish part of the country and those of the Irish Gaels who had settled themselves on the western seaboard. Within the Church itself, there was the normal tide of enthusiasm and subsequent relaxation, to be followed again by reform movements like the Céili Dé. There were the usual rackets: big centres of pilgrimage tried to attract more pilgrims and therefore income and some of the later hagiography is written with this intent, the local saint is represented as able to work miracles for everyone, even of the most unedifying kinds. Then the individual Celtic saint had his own particular troubles—perhaps in a man of royal descent like Columcille a savage pride in his high birth and a tendency to push people around, the kind of disposition that brought about the quarrel between him and St. Finbarr of Moville over the copy that Columcille made of Finbarr's newly-imported version of the Gospels, and which ended in a bloody battle between the saints' respective supporters. Or again, there might be opposition from the saint's own people to his following his vocation; the account of Columbanus is of his stepping over his mother when she threw herself across the threshold of their home to try and prevent his setting out to become a monk.

These were the normal internal troubles of Celtic Ireland and the Celtic saints. Added to them were the Viking attacks spread over a long period, and a constant strain on the nerves of anybody living within reach of their longships; a time when men looked ruefully on a bright moonlit night, as they did in the early days of the raids on Britain in the Second World War.

Abroad, the Celtic missionaries found themselves involved in the kind of difficulties that are only too familiar to us today, wickedness in high places in the warring states of Europe, the attempt to keep the Church out of politics, and if men like Columbanus continued to denounce the situation, the "rigged" trial and faked accusations against a too unyielding bishop like Desiderius and the expulsion from the country and from his monastery of Columbanus. The ship that should have taken Columbanus back to Ireland was driven ashore by a storm, and he stayed on the continent to continue his work in other territories more friendly to him than that of Theuderic of Burgundy. That did not end his adventures, for his journeys took him into really pagan areas, and finally, to Bobbio where the saint died, in which district the Arian heresy was rife amongst the people, and also apparently accepted by their king.

Indeed, if we go looking for troubles, for difficulties, for evils, in Celtic times, we are not long in finding plenty. In fact, there is an Irish treatise on the abuses of the times, composed sometime after 600 and before 725, a treatise that was widely known in Europe and seems, by its treatment of the subject of the unjust king, to have influenced European political thought on that topic. The treatise, *De Duodecim abusivis saeculi*, gives a list of twelve categories of bad men; categories not peculiar to Celtic times but familiar to all ages. Their titles read :— the wise man without works; the old man without religion; the youth without obedience; the rich man without alms-giving; the woman without chastity; the nobleman without virtue; the Christian who is quarrelsome; the poor man who is proud; the king who is unjust; the bishop who neglects his duty; the people without discipline; and the nation without law.

We are well aware of such evils today, both around us and in ourselves. It is so easy to be wise but never put your wisdom into action; to call yourself Christian and quarrel violently with the neighbour next door; to be poor and proud, or to be rich and neglect the responsibilities that riches bring. And if we try to pray, our thoughts go wandering off on a thousand and one different paths, none of them relevant to the matter in hand. The Celtic saints had the same experience :—

"Shame to my thoughts, how they stray from me! I dread great danger from it on the day of lasting Doom.

During the psalms they wander on a path that is not right : they run, they disturb, they misbehave before the eyes of great God.

Through eager assemblies, through companies of wanton women, through woods, through cities—swifter they are than the wind.

Now through ways of loveliness, and of riotous shame—no falsehood!

Without a ferry or a false step they go across every sea : swiftly they leap in one bound from earth to heaven.

They run—not a course of great wisdom—near, afar : along paths of great folly they reach their home.

Though one should try to bind them or put shackles on their feet, they are neither constant nor mindful to take a spell of rest.

Neither sword edge nor swish of lash will keep them down strongly; as slippery as an eel's tail they glide out of my grasp.

Neither lock or firm-vaulted dungeon, nor any fetter on earth, stronghold nor sea nor black fastness restrains them from their course.

O beloved truly chaste Christ, to whom every eye is clear, may the grace of the seven-fold Spirit come to keep them, to check them!

Rule this heart of mine, O swift God of the elements, that Thou mayst be my love, that I may do Thy will!

That I may reach Christ with His chosen companions, that we may be together : *they* are neither fickle nor inconstant—not as I am."

That 10th century Irish poem on the flightiness of thought from the Leabhar Breac brings us closer to the ordinary, everyday problems of Celtic prayer, the same problems as we experience ourselves. So too, the Céili Dé of Tallaght held that one should always recite the psalms from the written psalter; which had the threefold effect of restraining the three adversaries of one's attention, eye, tongue and wandering thoughts.

It is hard to realise the existence of these day to day difficulties of the Celtic monks, to avoid seeing the past through the wrong end of the telescope and failing to understand that a day and a week and a year took just as long to live through as they do today. It is easy to read of a bad man repenting in Celtic times and getting a seven-year stretch of penance; hard to understand that seven years was just as long then as now, that he faced not only austerity but boredom and the weariness of keeping on at the same thing day in day out.

But to understand the real significance of the attitude and devotion of the Celtic saints with which this book has been concerned, it is essential to grasp the background, that the Celts were like ourselves in their ordinary reactions to life, and that they did not live in a gilded paradise, but often enough faced evil and sin in violent forms just as we do now. Life has never been lived continuously on the peaks of contemplation.

Is it possible to penetrate still deeper into the spiritual life of the Celtic monks, to try and track the intimate details of their route to God? To some extent it can be done, though there was no Celtic St. John of the Cross to describe their ascent of Mount Carmel. The sources are two-fold:—a reading between the lines of the specifically Celtic turns of prayer and devotion, which this book has attempted to describe, coupled with the writings on prayer and the spiritual life common to the Church as a whole, particularly the summings up of Cassian and St. Gregory. From these, one gets an impression of a quite different route up the mountain from that of the Spanish mystics: they are both climbing to the same summit but they go by entirely different ways; I have the impression of St. John of the Cross picking a line up a gully whilst the Celtic saints kept out in the sunshine on the open hillside.

By the time that St. Ignatius Loyola was writing his "Spiritual Exercises" and, later, when St. John of the Cross and St. Teresa of Avila were detailing the mystic's way to God, men were in a much more introspective frame of mind than they had been in the earlier centuries of the Church. They wanted to watch themselves at a particular job and understand how they did it; earlier, the emphasis had been rather on the job than on the worker's reactions to it. So that the later writers on the spiritual life tend to be introspective, on what happens to the soul, whilst the earlier ones are more extrovert with the emphasis rather on the objective business of coming closer to God.

You feel this contrast again and again. Teresa of Avila writes in her "Life" about giving up all the world for God, almost wrenching oneself free from it in the first stages, but later coming to regret that the world was not more attractive than it is, so that one could have given up even more for the love of God. This is the way of negation, of turning away from everything that is not God; the Celtic saints on the other hand took the more sunlit route of affirmation, of mounting up to the Lord by means of His creation. For the Celtic saint, there was renunciation and penance, but not exactly that kind of renunciation of the Spanish mystical writers. He did turn entirely to God but he did not spurn His creation so entirely—rather saw it as a constant reminder of Him. St. Teresa turns sharply away from the beauty of the world to the beauty of God, Celtic Ireland used the one to reach the other. The world around us brings us reminders of the world to come, according to a 9th century Irish homily :—"There are, moreover, likenesses of the kingdom of heaven and of hell in this world. The likeness of hell therein, first, *i.e.*, winter and snow, tempest and cold, age and decay, disease and death. The likeness of the kingdom of heaven therein, however, summer and fair weather, blossom and leaf, beauty and youth, feasts and feastings, prosperity and abundance of every good."

There is another point to be considered too in mapping out the progress of a person's prayer and that is the person's environment. Certain things must take place in their spiritual life, they must come to cling entirely to God and detach themselves from other, hindering, loves and attachments, but the way in which they are brought about will vary with each individual and his circumstances. A nun in the quiet of a Carmelite convent will come to God through the dark nights of interior trials and desolations of which St. John of the Cross wrote, but the same results may be brought about in the soul of the bus driver rather by the sharp experience of his own work and life. The Celtic monks, with their monastic background but roving activities in the world, would tend to combine a little of both extremes in their lives, though all the while one has the feeling of positive action about them, of violent men fighting their way into heaven. We must all cross the desert, but there are different ways of doing it, passive endurance or the positive relish of the explorer.

The spiritual life then, had in Celtic times been much less analysed in terms of its effects on the individual soul, than nowadays. The way to God was just as hard, but men were less inclined to watch themselves walking along it. Today perhaps we have analysed too much and have too great a tendency to talk about our experiences at length from the psychiatrist's couch; we might do well to go back to that earlier simplicity of approach.

Formal meditation, which the modern handbook of prayer sets as the basis of the spiritual life, was unknown. Meditation, thinking about God, penetrating the mysteries of the scriptures, came much more simply : from the Mass, the Liturgy and from study of the Bible. The thoughts and phrases of the Divine Office lived with you; the desert fathers and the Celtic monks alike had psalms and other parts of scripture off by heart and said them at work in addition to their formal recitation in church. We tend today to set aside a fixed time for "meditation"; the Celtic method was to think about God at all times and in all places, and let the individual's meditation and prayer come as and when it would.

All periods of Church history seem to have their own particular private devotions—the Celtic Church had its "loricas" and its long litanies, it has been suggested that the Rosary took origin in Ireland with the Irish love of the Three Fifties, and they had some curious little devotional practices like the Céili Dé's "Shrine of Piety." That last consisted in praying in cross vigil to the four points of the compass in turn, at each reciting the Pater noster, and Deus in adjutorium meum intende : Domine, ad adjuvandum me festina, three times. Over and above the official liturgy, there was already a Catholic variety of private devotions in being to suit different temperaments.

Against this background, we can go back to the teaching of Abbot Pinufius in the desert, that the spiritual life begins with the fear of the Lord and rises up therefrom to the wisdom of contemplation and apostolic love. It seems to me that a question put to the Celtic saints about the stages of the spiritual life would have got that kind of answer rather than the more subjective one that was to be given later by St. John of the Cross. St. Augustine in his commentary on the Sermon on the Mount puts the whole concept very concisely, setting the first seven Beatitudes (the 8th, he says, really repeats and comes back to the first) against the seven gifts of the Holy Spirit detailed by Isaias and the seven petitions of the Lord's Prayer, combining them into the seven stages of the spiritual life.

We begin then, with the fear of the Lord, for this is the beginning of wisdom. It is linked up with humility and the poor in spirit who will gain the kingdom of heaven. Today, the phrase "fear of the Lord" implies a servile fear, a superstitious sanction of hell fire. Actually, it is something very different; it means belief and faith that God exists and from that basic fact, that He is in control of the world and that the pattern of things have a meaning and purpose. It means too the consciousness of a definite hierarchy of being, of man fitted into a particular niche in the scheme of things, lord indeed of the beasts but lesser than the angels; it does imply humility but it also implies fitting into one's proper place and losing the sense of being caught up in a meaningless whirl of events. Belief in God, the fear of the Lord, is also the beginning of charity, we must know that God exists before we can love Him, or try to do His will.

From the fear of the Lord, we move on to godliness, piety, the meek who will inherit the land. At this stage, there is study of scripture, and a certain meekness in the student in not condemning passages in it out of hand because he is not yet able to penetrate their meaning. Knowledge very naturally follows from this work of study, and the realisation of the evils and sins in which the soul is still involved. "Blessed are they that mourn," the individual begins to grieve after God, and then, to turn to Him and abandon his excessive love of created things. This marks the fourth stage, of fortitude and hungering and thirsting after justice. Next comes counsel—we are being shown how to put that hungering and thirsting into effective action, and learning to forgive as we hope to be forgiven, "blessed are the merciful." From counsel, to purity of heart and understanding; only as we work free of our sins and vices and come close to God do we really begin to understand. And finally, to wisdom itself, to the contemplation of the truth, becoming like God and penetrated by His peace :—"Blessed are the peacemakers, for they shall be called the children of God."

By these stages then, we can climb up from the valley of tears to the mountain of peace, from our first tentative efforts at prayer to contemplation of God. We believe that God exists and we begin to try and learn about Him from the scriptures and to root out our faults. St. Gregory in the "Morals," speaking of a daily examination of conscience, uses the pleasant metaphor of the flame of love on the altar of our hearts being refueled daily by our studies of scripture and of the saints, and then burning up our sins. And as we come to know more and understand more, the hunger and thirst for God increases, and with it, distress at our continued shortcomings and our inability to do as much as we want to for God. The Celtic ideal of white martyrdom is not an academic theory, it expresses a need in the life of every saint. "The more the sound of inward wisdom by the grace of its secret inspiration bursts upon us, the more does it affect us with distress. For no one would outwardly lament that which he is, if he had not been able to perceive within, that which as yet he is not." (St. Gregory: "Morals on the Book of Job").

Contemplation here on earth in fact, always has a bitter sweet tang about it. Our whole nature craves for truth, to know it and delight in it; in so far, as by infused contemplation we are brought close to Truth itself, we experience happiness, but in so far as we realise that this hidden contact on earth falls short of the direct vision of heaven, we remain mourning and weeping in the valley of tears with unsatisfied longing. We are still pilgrims on the road, crossing the desert to the Land of Promise.

In very brief outline, this appears to me to be the basic lines on which the spiritual life of the Celtic monks was laid down. It has about it the simplicity of the 33rd Psalm, but it is a simplicity that includes all the essentials :—

"Venite filii, audite me : timorem Domini docebo vos.

Prohibe linguam tuam a malo : et labia tua ne loquantur dolum. Diverte a malo, et fac bonum : inquire pacem, et persequere eam.

Juxta est Dominus iis, qui tribulatio sunt corde : et humiles spiritu salvabit.

Redimet Dominus animas servorum suorum : et non delinquent omnes qui sperant in eo."

It is as simple—and as hard, as that, the turning from evil to good. Nor must we forgot in the heat of the conflict and struggle that it is God Who loved us first, and that He is both our objective and our constant helper and protector here and now. So then, the 9th century Irish homily already quoted, concludes with a description of the Lord that the Celtic saints served and sought and loved, and of the kingdom to which they were trying to make their way :—

"Blessed is he who shall reach the kingdom where is God Himself, a king, great, fair, powerful, strong, holy, pure, righteous, keen, merciful, charitable, beneficent, old, young, wise, noble, glorious, without beginning, without end, without age, without decay. May we arrive at the kingdom of that King, may we merit it, may we inhabit it, in saecula saeculorum. Amen."

Chapter Fourteen

CONCLUSION

So then, looking back to the Celtic saints, and trying to piece together their outlook upon life, there is an impression of integration, of men and women who saw unity and meaning in the diversity of the world, just as the strands of the interwoven patterns of Celtic art thread in and out. The Celtic artist had the feel of the completed design, he knew where each strand reappeared and knotted in with the next; for us today that sense of pattern and design seems lost, we turn from one thing to the next without a sense of their relationship one to the other.

The modern city presents us with a thousand and one conflicting attractions; by night the neon advertisements flash in opposition to the winking traffic lights, the cinema screaming louder than the controls for the glittering lines of cars. Our senses are inevitably diverted, drawn away first to one thing and then the other, away from the basic meaning and shape of life, away from the stark essentials, the bread and water in the desert, into a jungle of luxuries, inessential gadgets, technical marvels. We mask our deep-seated craving to know where we are going and why and what for, in rushing from one amusement to the next, in pleasure in a new electrical device, or, at a deeper level, in doing good, in a hectic round of activity in social service.

The tendency is to concentrate upon the here and now, upon immediate results, in cash if possible. The stress falls more and more upon "vocational" training; our first reaction to a proposed piece of research is to consider its commercial value; it is no longer possible for a poet to live by his art and its rewards. Mystery and symbol have lost their meaning; our interest concentrates upon the brash and standardised products coming off the factory conveyer belts and the possession of these things.

And yet with all our technical knowledge and our research, we walk blindfold, holding off the future at arm's length, fighting down the thought of death with that of the modern doctor's control of disease and screening the thought of eternity with the bright corridors of the modern hospital.

Against that outlook, the Celtic saints stand out in stark contrast; men to whom death was not the end but the entry into new and fuller life and activity, something to which the whole of life led up, and which should be looked forward to and welcomed. Yet that attitude did not mean turning away from the world, seeking "pie in the sky" and leaving the people to starve here on earth. Rather it gave meaning to life here, because every action was related to eternity, the evil that was done could lead to hell, the good to heaven, a man must watch his step if he is not to mistake the road. Nor does the Christian outlook imply the need to abandon the city and its inventions for a crude peasant settlement—the Celtic level of scholarship, of technical achievement in metallurgy, in art, and in seamanship, give the lie to that idea. All these things can be integrated, brought into the pattern of life, if once the key to the design is discovered.

It is, in the phrase of the Irish authors, "not hard to tell" what did enable the Celtic saints to achieve this integration. It was their belief in God and in the Incarnation and Resurrection.

That belief, if it is not a mere pious lip service, puts the whole of life in a new context, both for the individual and for the world around him. He is no longer walking in darkness, not knowing where he is going, he has an objective and is being given the means, if he will make use of them, to attain it. The world becomes meaningful, no longer a jumble of events, and God is seen in control above all the conflicting whirlpools and eddies of history. But this does not mean that the Christian will stand aloof from the day to day problems of the world, though he may be less distressed by them in the sense that he believes in the Fall and in original sin and is therefore more tolerant of human failings and sins; it is in the creature's nature and the perfect race is not to be bred here. Again, we can look to the Celtic saints, whose activities were so often political and whose opponents must have indeed often wished that their interests had been entirely concentrated in heaven. Life on earth is complementary to life in eternity; the pattern of the one will determine the pattern of the other.

Moreover, belief in the Gospels, means a completion, a rounding off, of our view of the world. We are no longer brought up with a jerk, like a dog on the end of a chain, halting our knowledge of reality with material things; we become conscious of spiritual values and realities that complete the picture and give it meaning.

This, in fact, is the paradox of Christianity, that to secure your life you must lose it, the total giving that ends in inheriting the earth. The complete turning to God of the Celtic saints, the violence of their ideal of penance and white martyrdom ended in making them freemen of the world, who could enjoy and handle and direct its affairs without becoming enslaved by them.

It is not an easy road, however. If we, in our modern technological civilisation, attempt to integrate the pattern by the methods of the saints, we shall come up against the problems of the saints. Christianity is a guarantee of happiness in the world to come, but not of comfort and ease in this; the Church on earth is a fighting army. The high cross carvings of the temptation of St. Anthony are no mere salute to the success of a gallant soldier; they indicate what we must all expect if we venture out into the desert. The easy-going, come day go day, of the materialist, is abandoned for a purposeful journey, in which every word and action counts and their effects carefully considered beforehand.

Can we, to help ourselves in the reintegration of our lives, recover our lost sense of symbol? Can we, in fact, come back to understand the mysterious symbolism of basic things like bread and water and from them, penetrate more deeply into the meaning of the Church's sacraments? It seems that we must attempt to do so, that a sense of symbolism is as part of a normal human mind, a prop of sanity. But it is not easy to do so; circled by all our variety of good things, it is hard to pick out the essentials for life: here the primitive peasant has the advantage of the townsman, for the bread and wine of the Mass, the water of baptism, are immediately related to the basic needs of his physical existence. Yet the townsman can surely attempt to distinguish more clearly between the essential and the inessential in the things that are offered him to buy, to search into the roots of things. These basic things are symbols for all time, but others, the Bestiary animals for example, relate to particular cultures and particular states of knowledge of the world. Each civilisation ought, to be healthy, to throw up a crop of symbols of its own; we ought to look for meaning in our own, in the jet plane trailing vapour across the clear sky, in the thrill of speed in a fast car on the open road. If we but use them right, these things can lead us deeper into understanding of the meaning of the world. We need to resist the temptation to reject all knowledge that cannot be checked by scientific experiment, to make it possible for the writing of poetry to be a gainful occupation once more.

It seems that the experience of the Celtic saints can give us a lead on the road we should take ; their prayer springing simply and easily from the liturgy and the scriptures and becoming their source of power and activity in the world. With that uncomplicated approach to God, went a vivid realisation of the interpenetration of material things by spiritual ones, a sense of reality about angels and demons, and of community with the saints in heaven. It is this sense particularly that we have lost—the feeling for the meaning of symbols stems from it— and that we should strive to regain. We do not really, even if we call ourselves Christian, in the least believe that a single sin is far more evil than all the world's material ills and injustices ; we do not really see the Mass as something more vital, more essential, to our existence and well-being than all the concerns that surge around the Church, from those in our own home to international relations.

Nor do we realise the power of prayer ; it is perhaps something said mechanically, or a request programme of our immediate needs. We have lost our sense of being meaningful units in the mystical body of Christ ; we ought to see our prayer as part of the design to bring the grace of God to men, and understand that when we pray, we are linking up and co-operating with His power and omnipotence, and that that power and omnipotence is something real.

In fact, this study of the Celtic saints and of their spiritual life, must always bring us back to where we began, to the praying figure on the Bantry pillar stone and to the two old hermits and the bread from heaven on the cross of Nigg. In these things lies the key to the Celtic saints' successful integration and organisation of their lives, in prayer and in the Mass, and in the concept of life as a pilgrimage across the desert to the Land of Promise.

APPENDIX

The date of the Antiphonary is fixed by those of the individuals listed in the hymn "In Memory of Our Abbots" as between 680 and 691. The book contains the following items :—

1. 6 Canticles :—
   Canticum Moysi. "Audite caeli quae loquor."
   Benedictio Sancti Zachariae. "Benedictus Dominus Deus."
   Canticum (Moysi). "Cantemus Domino gloriose."
   Benedictio (trium) puerorum. "Benedicite omnia opera."
   Ymnum in die dominica. "Te Deum."
   Ad vesperum et admatutinam. "Gloria in excelsis."

2. 12 Metrical hymns :—
   Ymnum S. Hilari de Christo. "Ymnum dicat turba fr(atrum)."
   Ymnum Apostolorum, ut alii dicunt. "Praecamur Patrem."
   Ymnum quando communicarent sacerdotes. "Sancti venite Christus corpus."
   Ymnum quando caeria benedicitur. "Ignis creator igneus."
   Ymnum mediae noctis. "Mediae noctis tempus est."
   Ymnum in natale martyrym vel sabbeto ad matutinum. "Sacratissimi martyres."
   Ymnum ad matutinam in dominica. "Spirito divinae lucis."
   Ymnum S. Patrici magister Scotorum. "Audite omnis amantes."
   Ymnum S. Comgilli abbatis nostri. "Recordemur iustitiae."
   Ymnum S. Camelaci. "Audite bonum exemplum."
   Versiculi familiae Benchuir. "Benchuir bona regula."
   (In) memoriam abbatum nostrorum. "Sancta sanctorum opera."

3. 69 collects for use at the Canonical hours.

4. 17 collects for use for particular people or on particular occasions.

5. 70 anthems and versicles.

6. The Creed.

7. The Pater noster.

From the Antiphonary of Bangor.
The Hymn in honour of the Martyrs.

Sacratissimi martyres summi Dei,
Bellatores fortissimi Christi regis,
Potentissimi duces exercitus Dei,
Victores in coelis Deo canentes,

Alleluia.

Excelsissime Christe coelorum Deus,
Cherubin cui sedes cum Patre sacra,
Angelorum ibi et martyrum fulgens chorus
Tibi sancti proclamant,

Alleluia.

Magnifice tu prior omnium passus crucem,
Qui devicta morte refulsisti mundo,
Ascendisti ad coelos ad dexteram Dei,
Tibi sancti proclamant,

Alleluia.

Armis spiritalibus munita mente
Apostoli sancti te sunt secuti,
Qui cum ipsam crucis paterentur mortem
Tibi sancti canebant,

Alleluia.

Christe, martyrum tu es adjutor potes
Proeliantium sancta pro tua gloria,
Qui cum victories exirent de hoc saeculo,
Tibi sancti canebant,

Alleluia.

Illustris tua, Domine, laudanda virtus
Quae per Spiritum Sanctum firmavit martyres,
Qui consternerent zabulum et mortem vincerent
Tibi sancti canebant,

Alleluia.

Manu Domini excelsa protecti
Contra diabolum steterunt firmati,
Semper Trinitati fidem toto cordo servantes,
Tibi sancti canebant.

                                        Alleluia.

Vere regnantes erant tecum, Christe Deus
Qui passionis merito coronas habent
Et centenario fructu repleti gaudent,
Tibi sancti proclamant,

                                        Alleluia.

Christi Dei gratiam supplices obsecramus
Ut in ipsius gloriam consummemur
Et in sanctam Jerusalem civitatem Dei
Trinitati cum sanctis dicamus,

                                        Alleluia.

FROM THE ANTIPHONARY OF BANGOR.
HYMNUS AD MATUTINEM IN DOMINICA.

Spiritus divinae lucis gloriae.

                    Respice in me, Domine.

Deus veritatis,
Domine Deus Sabaoth,
Deus Israel.

                    Respice in me, Domine.

Lumen de lumine,
Referemus Filium Patris,
Sanctumque Spiritum in una substantia.

                    Respice in me, Domine.

Unigenitus et primogenitus
A te obtinemus
Redemptionem nostram.

                    Respice in me, Domine.

Natus es Sancto Spiritu
Ex Maria Virgine,
In id ipsum in adoptionem
Filiorum qui tibi
Procreati ex fonte vivunt.

                    Respice in me, Domine.

Heredes et coheredes
Christi tui, in quo
Et per quem cuncta creasti,
Quia in praedestinatione
A saeculis nobis est
Deus Jesu, qui nunc coepit.

                              Respice in me, Domine.

Unigenito ex mortuis
Deo obtinens corpus
Claritatem Dei, manens
In saecula saeculorum
Rex aeternorum.

                              Respice in me, Domine.

Quia nunc coepit qui semper fuit,
Naturae tuae Filius,
Divinae lucis gloriae tuae,
Qui est forma et plenitudo
Divinitatis tuae frequens,

                              Respice in me, Domine.

Persona unigeniti
Et primogeniti
Qui est totus a toto
Diximus lux de lumine,

                              Respice in me, Domine.

Et Deum verum a Deo
Vero sese confitemur
Tribus personis
In una substantia.

                              Respice in me, Domine.

The following collect may have been intended for use with the hymn :—

Sancte Domine, illuminatio et salus vera credentibus, resurrectio dominicae
claritatis, illumina cor nostrum, ut Trinitatis scientia, et Unitatis cognitione,
filii lucis, et membra Christi, ac templum Sancti Spiritus esse mereamur,
Qui regnas in saecula saeculorum.

Hymn of Colman Mac Mur-chon to St. Michael.

In Trinitate spes mea fixa non in omine
et archangelum deprecor Michaelem nomine.

Ut sit obvius ac misus mihi deo doctore
hora exitus de vita ista atque corpore.

Ne me ducat in amarum minister inergiae
ipse princeps tenebrarum atque pes superbiae.

Adjutorium succurrat Michaelis et Archangeli
ad me hora qua gaudebunt justi atque angeli.

Illum rogo ne demittat mihi truces species
inimici sed deducat ubi regni requies.

Adiuvat me sanctus Michael diebus ac noctibus
ut me ponat in bonorum sanctorum consortibus.

Sanctus Michael intercedat adiutor probalis
pro me quia sum peccator actu atque fragilis.

Sanctus Michael me defendat semper suis viribus
anima egrediente cum sanctorum milibus.

Sanctus Gabriel, sanctus Raphiel atque omnes angeli
intercedant pro me semper simul et archangeli.

Eterna possint prestare regis regni aulia
ut possedeam cum Christo paradisi gaudia.

Gloria sit semper deo patri atque filio
simul cum spiritu sancto in uno consilio.

———

Adjuvat nos archangelus sanctus Michael dignissimus
quem recipere animas mittat deus altissimus.

METRICAL TRANSLATION OF THE HYMN OF ST. CÚ-CHUIMNE IN HONOUR OF OUR LADY.

In alternate measure chanting, daily sing we Mary's praise,
And in strains of glad rejoicing, to the Lord our voices raise.

With a twofold choir repeating Mary's never dying fame,
Let each ear the praises gather, which our grateful tongues proclaim.

Juda's ever glorious daughter—chosen mother of the Lord—
Who, to weak and fallen manhood all its ancient worth restored.

From the everlasting Father, Gabriel brought the glad decree,
That the Word Divine conceiving, she should set poor sinners free.

Of all virgins pure, the purest,—ever stainless, ever bright—
Still from grace to grace advancing—fairest daughter of the light.

Wondrous title—who shall tell it—whilst the Word divine she bore
Though in mother's name rejoicing, virgin purer than before!

By a woman's disobedience, eating the forbidden tree,
Was the world betray'd and ruin'd—was by woman's aid set free.

In mysterious mode a mother, Mary did her God conceive,
By whose grace, through saving waters, men did heav'nly truth receive.

By no empty dreams deluded, for the pearl which Mary bore
Men, all earthly wealth resigning, still are rich for evermore.

For her Son a seamless tunic Mary's careful hand did weave;
O'er that tunic fiercely gambling, sinners Mary's heart did grieve.

Clad in helmet of salvation—clad in breastplate shining bright—
May the hand of Mary guide us to the realms of endless light.

Amen, amen, loudly cry we—may she when the fight is won,
O'er avenging fires triumphing, lead us safely to her Son.

Holy angels gathering round us, lo, His saving name we greet,
Writ in books of life eternal, may we still that name repeat.

This translation was made by the Rev. Professor Potter of Dublin and published in Cardinal Moran's "Essays on the Early Irish Church" (Dublin, 1864).

Hymn of St. Oengus Mac Tipraite in honour of St. Martin.

From the Irish Liber Hymnorum. Oengus Mac Tipraite died 746. The hymn is an example of early Irish devotion to St. Martin, and seems to have been used as a lorica, for the Preface to it says it is a protection "against every disease, and heaven for reciting it on lying down and rising up."

Martine te deprecor pro me rogaris patrem
Christum ac spiritum sanctum
habentem Mariam matrem.

Martinus mirus more ore laudavit deum
puro corde cantavit atque amavit eum.

Electus dei vivi signa sibi salutis
donavit deus pacis magnae atque virtutis.

Verbum dei locutus secutus in mandatis
virtutibus impletis mortuis resuscitatis.

Sanans homines lepra cura duplica mira
magnitudine mala egretudina dira.

Deum dominum nostrum passum pro nobis mire
voluntarie propter nos deprecare Martine.

———

Sanctus Martinus adhuc catacominus hac me veste contexit dicit dominus omnipotens.

Per merita Martini
Sancti atque dignissimi
nos precamur
ut mereamur
regnum dei vivi altissimi.   Amen.

REFERENCES TO LITERATURE

The following references are not intended as a complete bibliography but rather as an indication of books which contain such complete lists, of books giving accounts of the history and development of the Celtic Church, and of some published editions of the Celtic literature quoted in the present work.

Allen, J. Romilly, and Anderson, J.: "The Early Christian Monuments of Scotland." Edinburgh. Society of Antiquaries of Scotland, 1903.

Athanasius, St.: "The Life of St. Antony." Translated by Robert T. Meyer. Longmans, Green & Co., London, 1950, being Vol. 10 in Ancient Christian Writers series.

Bangor, Antiphonary of: Henry Bradshaw Society, London, 1893. 2 vols.

Bieler, Ludwig: "The Life and Legend of St. Patrick." Dublin. Clonmore and Reynolds, 1949.

Cassian, John: The Institutes of the Coenobia and the Conferences. Translated by E. C. S. Gibson. In Nicene & Post-Nicene Fathers of the Christian Church series. Oxford, 1894.

Day of Judgment, Irish poem on: Translated by J. G. O'Keeffe. *Eriu*, Vol. III, 1907, pp. 29-33.

Donatus, Sr. M.: "Beasts and Birds in the Lives of the Early Irish Saints." Philadelphia. 1934.

Félire Huí Gormáin. The Martyrology of Gorman: Text and translation. Henry Bradshaw Society, London, 1895.

Félire Oéngusso Céili Dé. The Martyrology of Oengus the Culdee: Text and translation. Henry Bradshaw Society, London, 1905.

Fragment of an Old Irish Treatise on the Psalter: Edited by Kuno Meyer. Anecdota Oxoniensia Hibernica Minora. Oxford, 1894.

Gougaud, Louis: "Christianity in Celtic Lands." Sheed & Ward, London, 1932.

Henry, Françoise: "Irish Art in the Early Christian Period." London. Methuen, 1940.

Irish Liber Hymnorum: Henry Bradshaw Society, London, 1898. 2 vols.

Irish Litanies: Henry Bradshaw Society, London, 1925.

Kenny, James F.: "The Sources for the Early History of Ireland." Vol. I. Ecclesiastical. New York. Columbia University Press, 1929. This is a most important source book, giving full lists of all extant Celtic MSS. and their published editions.

Leabhar Breac: The Passions, Homilies and Legends in Vols. II and VI of the Todd Lecture Series of the Royal Irish Academy, Dublin, 1887 and 1895. The Irish Tract on the Mass in translation in the *Irish Ecclesiastical Record* for 1866, pp. 170-179. The poem on the Flightiness of Thought, edited and translated by Kuno Meyer in *Eriu*, Vol. III, 1907, pp. 13-15.

McNeill, John T., and Gamer, Helena M.: "Medieval Handbooks of Penance." A translation of the principal "libri poenitentiales" and selections from related documents. Columbia University Press, 1938.

Meyer, Kuno: "Selections from Ancient Irish Poetry." London. Constable & Co., 1913.

Mould, D. D. C. Pochin: "Ireland of the Saints." London. Batsford, 1953. "Scotland of the Saints." London. Batsford, 1952. "Irish Pilgrimage." Dublin. 1955.

O'Briain, Felim: "Irish Missionaries and Medieval Church Reform." *Miscellanea Historica Alberti De Meyer*, pp. 228-254. Louvain, 1946, "The Blessed Eucharist in Irish Liturgy & History." *Studia Eucharistica*, pp. 216-245. Antwerp, 1946. "The Expansion of Irish Christianity." *Irish Historical Studies*, Vol. III (1943), pp. 241-266, and Vol. IV (1944). pp. 131-163.

Patrick, St.: "Confession" and "Letter to the Soldiers of Coroticus." Translated by Ludwig Bieler. London. Longmans, Green & Co., 1953, being No. 17 in Ancient Christian Writers series. This volume also contains the Lorica of St. Patrick and St. Secundinus' Hymn on St. Patrick.

Rules of Irish Saints: Ailbe of Emly, *Eriu*, Vol. III, 1907, pp. 92-115. Carthage, *Irish Ecclesiastical Record*, Vol. 27, 4th series, 1910, pp. 495-517 Columba. Translation only in W. F. Skene's "Celtic Scotland.". Edinburgh, 1877, Vol. II, pp. 508-9. Comgall, *Eriu*, Vol. I, 1904, pp. 191-208. Rule of the Monastery of Tallaght. Edited by Edward Gwynn. Hermathena, No. 44, 2nd supplemental volume, Dublin, 1927.

Ryan, John: "Irish Monasticism." Dublin. Talbot Press, 1931.

Severus, Sulpicius: "The Life of St. Martin." "Two Dialogues."

Simpson, W. Douglas: "The Celtic Church in Scotland." Aberdeen. The University Press, 1935. "The Historical St. Columba." Aberdeen, Milne & Hutchison, 2nd edition, 1927. "St. Ninian and the origins of the Christian Church in Scotland." Edinburgh. Oliver & Boyd, 1940.

Stowe Missal: Henry Bradshaw Society, London, 1906.

Tallaght, Martyrology of: Henry Bradshaw Society, London, 1931.

Tallaght, The Monastery of: E. J. Gwynn and W. J. Purton in Proceedings of the Royal Irish Academy, Vol. 29, C. 1911, pp. 115-179.

Thesaurus Palaeohibernicus: Edited by Whitley Stokes and John Strachan. Cambridge, 1903, Vol. II. A collection of Old Irish glosses, scholia, prose and verse. Includes the Cambrai Homily, Tract on the Mass from the Stowe Missal, Colman's Hymn, Sanctan's Hymn, etc.

INDEX